PRAISE FOR

Case Critical

In this insightful and very readable book, Ben Carniol cuts through layers of neo-conservative misconceptions to show that unfair advantage, not talent, accounts for the ever-rising inequality in our society. *Case Critical* has become an essential primer on social justice – and injustice – in Canada.   — **Linda McQuaig**, author and journalist

Ben Carniol shares the voices of the people and the helpers, and connects us with a multitude of resources: writings, organizations, and community experiences. A must-read for all those engaged in developing their own understandings and their own best practices.
            — **Jim Albert**, First Nations Elder and social work educator

Ben Carniol's *Case Critical* has been an assigned reading in my social work classes for many years. Each new edition enlightens, inspires, provokes – and always results in critical examination and reflection on social work practice.
            — **Elizabeth Radian**, Social Work, Red Deer College, Alberta

Ben has done a superb job. . . . He understands the history and struggles of Indigenous peoples in Canada.
— **Yvonne Howse**, Indian Social Work,
First Nations University of Canada

Case Critical is a must-read for anyone working within the social services sector in Canada.
— **Bob Mullaly**, Social Work, University of Manitoba

Case Critical honestly presents the oppressive realities of social services in Canada while simultaneously engendering a sense of hope and possibility. First-person accounts from workers and clients inform Carniol's astute analysis, and the extended discussions of privilege and activism are especially welcome additions.
— **Carolyn Campbell**, Social Work, Dalhousie University

This book will inform and inspire a new generation of social workers in Canada to become more self-reflective, able to recognize oppressive policies and practices in the agencies in which they work, and prepared to engage in social justice efforts inside and outside the profession.   — **Shari Brotman**, Social Work, McGill University

Case Critical
Social Services & Social Justice in Canada

Sixth Edition

Ben Carniol

Between the Lines
Toronto, Canada

Case Critical, Sixth Edition

© 1987, 1990, 1995, 2000, 2005, 2010 Ben Carniol

First published in Canada by
Between the Lines
401 Richmond Street West, Studio 277
Toronto ON M5V 3A8
Canada

1-800-718-7201
www.btlbooks.com

Library and Archives Canada Cataloguing in Publication

Carniol, Ben
        Case critical : social services and social justice in Canada / Ben Carniol. – 6th ed.
Includes bibliographical references.
ISBN 978-1-897071-65-6

1. Social service – Canada.   2. Social workers – Canada.   I. title
HV105.C39 2010   361.3′0971   C2010-904563-7

Front cover image courtesy of The Door Store
Cover design based on *Case Critical* Fifth Edition cover by Lancaster Reid Creative
Interior design and page preparation by Steve Izma
Printed in Canada
Third printing January 2014

RECYCLED
Paper made from
recycled material
FSC   FSC® C103567
www.fsc.org

Between the Lines gratefully acknowledges assistance for its publishing activities from the Canada Council for the Arts, the Ontario Arts Council, the Government of Ontario through the Ontario Book Publishers Tax Credit program and through the Ontario Book Initiative, and the Government of Canada through the Canada Book Fund.

 Canada Council   Conseil des Arts
for the Arts   du Canada   Canadä    ONTARIO ARTS COUNCIL
CONSEIL DES ARTS DE L'ONTARIO

CONTENTS

PREFACE

This book is about the realities of both those who receive and those who deliver social services. It is about the influences that shape social services. It also seeks answers to troubling questions. Why are social problems getting worse? How can we reverse the prevailing social trends?

In the early 1980s, when I began work on what became the first edition of this book, it seemed to me that much of the writing about social services was remote from the realities. In the twenty years or more since then, social work education has narrowed the gap between theory and practice. Among other changes, more critical and progressive perspectives are now being taught by a new generation of social work educators who have taken up positions at colleges and universities. Today new and more progressive approaches about the delivery of Canadian social services and about social work practice are being researched, written about, and discussed in a growing number of articles, books, workshops, and conferences. Innovations in the field are increasingly being recognized.

Still, just when social work education is deepening and strengthening its progressive and critical approaches, many social services are moving in an opposite direction, to the detriment of service users – leaving us no choice but to ask: Why are so many social services contradicting their official purposes? What are the critical or progressive practices that are relevant to respectful and effective social work practice?

As part of the new generation of educators and practitioners in the field, Indigenous social work scholars are raising fundamental questions. Is mainstream social work and social services doing more harm than good in our communities? How can social services shed their colonialism? Many mainstream social work educators and practitioners are also asking questions. Why do so many of today's social services fail to provide effective help to people who need it? What can we do about the barriers that prevent the delivery of effective social services?

This new edition attempts to answer these critical questions and to place them in the context of the many innovations happening in the field today. In doing this work I have built on my own experience as a social service provider and social work educator that spans over forty-five years: just under twenty years spent in Cleveland, Montreal, and Calgary – and now over twenty-five years in Toronto. In documenting many of the innovations occurring today I am particularly grateful for having such a wide selection of studies and reports to draw upon. This edition also contains updated information, statistics, critical analysis, and new quotes from people who deliver and people who receive social services.

The original book's interviews, which were carried out during the early 1980s in Halifax, Toronto, Calgary, and Vancouver, were supplemented in subsequent editions. Special thanks go to these women, men, and in some cases children who agreed to be interviewed over the years and who sometimes took considerable risk in being candid and sharing painful realities. I am also grateful to the social workers who shed light on their work environments and the pressures of their jobs. In many cases their names remain anonymous to protect their positions. Excerpts from these interviews occur throughout the book in italics.

These pages will challenge readers. But then today's multiple injustices, with their global-to-local connections, are also quite challenging for the victims and survivors of these injustices. At the same time this book is also meant to offer hope. It provides examples of social services that are welcomed by service users. It shows how social workers are engaged in bringing social justice closer to reality. I have found that such engagement is not only feasible, practical, and necessary, but also carries its own rewards – among which is the chance to see some people receive the help they truly need.

It has been gratifying that for over twenty years now, through the various editions of this book, I have received continuous support and encouragement from my publishers, Between the Lines. Robert Clarke has provided superb and meticulous editorial guidance through all six editions of this project. With a sharp eye for the political implications of the evidence I was gathering, Robert helped me to clarify my perspective and my conclusions. My thanks go also to others at BTL, including Jennifer Tiberio, Paula Brill, and Steve Izma, who have guided the book through subsequent stages.

Julie Faubert of Ryerson's School of Social Work was generous in her response whenever I interrupted her work with questions about computer software glitches or barriers; she helped me clear a path to completion of the typescript for this edition. I also appreciate the supportive environment at the Ryerson School of Social Work, where aid was extended to me by many colleagues, including Jeff Edmunds, Jacquie Durand, Judith Sandys, Valerie Holder, Samantha Wehbi, Gordon Pon, Jennifer Clarke, Tara LaRose, Susan Preston, Akua Benjamin, Henry Parada, and Jennifer Poole.

Waubauno Kwe (Barbara Riley), Anishinaabe First Nations Elder from Walpole Island in Ojibway territory in Ontario, shared her cultural wisdom as she mentored and supported me during my journey of change as I learned about the healing ways of First Nations culture. Indigenous Elder and social work educator Jim Albert modelled ways of honouring identity and of discovering the inner knowledge and strength required to become good helpers.

Through the years the assistance of a number of Indigenous individuals from coast to coast in what is now called Canada in the northern part of Turtle Island enabled me to become an ally to Indigenous communities: Lynn Lavallée, Métis of Algonquin, Cree, and French heritage; Monica McKay, Nisga'a Nation; Ruth Koleszar-Green, Mohawk Nation from Haudenosaunee Confederacy and Territory; Malcolm Saulis, Maliseet Nation; Raven Sinclair, Cree/Assiniboine and Saulteaux from Gordon's and Kawacatoose First Nations; Cyndy Baskin of Mi'kmaw Nation and Irish descent; and Yvonne Howse, Cree Nation. From the Anishinaabe nations: Banakonda Kennedy-Kish (Bell), Gord Bruyere, Catherine Brooks, and Theresa Horan. From the Mohawk Nation: Heather Green, Brenda Sager, Mary Ann Spencer, Janice Hill, and Leslie Spenser.

In earlier editions Canadian feminist and social work educator Helen Levine provided me with detailed feedback and thereby helped to place the role of women and women's conditions and struggles at centre stage. Her suggestions helped me raise my consciousness around ways in which I could become an ally in the struggle for gender equality.

Dorothy Moore, a long-time friend and Adjunct Professor at Dalhousie University's Maritime School of Social Work, continued to provide valuable assistance as an ally in my work with networks of activists within the Canadian Association for Social Work Education. The Canadian Association of Social Workers and the Canadian Association for Social Work Education provided me with updated reports and statistics.

I want to thank Canadian Scholars' Press for allowing me to draw generously from one of their publications: a chapter, co-authored with Vivian Del Valle, that appeared in the book *Structural Social Work in Action: Examples from Practice* (2010), edited by Steven Hick, Heather Peters, Tammy Corner, and Tracy London.

It would take a separate volume to explain how everyone identified in this Preface (as well as many more people not listed here) contributed to my evolving analysis and social activism. My long-time friends from Jerusalem, Elliot Israel Cohen and Veronika Cohen, demonstrated local-global linkages in their intercommunal work with Christian and Muslim Palestinians and Israeli Jews who are seeking peace with justice for both Israelis and Palestinians. Closer to home, friends and colleagues provided me with supportive circles in our pursuit of social justice: Paul Agueci, Pari Aram, Patricia Alexander, Hannah Brown, Sam Blatt, Pam Chapman, Jim and Kathy Chang, Anne Clavir, Juergen Dankwort, Deborah Frenette, Harry Fox, Frieda Forman, Carolina Gana, Marcy Gilbert, Steven Hick, Joanne Jackson, Murray Grummitt, Brian Horychka, Ronnee Jaeger, Ellen Katz, Joel and Sonia Kurtz, Ilona Lampi, David Lesk, Heather MacDonald, Jim McCall, Tirza Meacham, Leonard Molczadski, Jill and Morris Moscovitch, Anne Moorhouse, Valerie Packota, Steve Pizzano, Beth Porter, Luisa Quarta, Elizabeth Radian, Baruch Rand, Luci Rice, Shalom Schachter, Jadie Schettino, Yaakov and

Tzila Schneid, Judy Tsao, Eileen Oi-Lin Wan, Sheri Weisberg, and Linda Zelicki.

Of utmost importance were the gifts of time, support, and understanding that I received from Rhona, my life partner, and our two adult daughters, Mira and Naomi. Without Rhona's ever-present affection, this project would not have been completed. Mira's and Naomi's contributions to make the world a better place affirm my sense that social justice is possible. My siblings and their families, as well as Rhona's parents and their family, have strengthened me through their heartfelt emotional support.

This book is dedicated to those in my immediate family who are no longer with us but whose spirit and love continue to be with me: my parents, Elsa and Mathias Carniol; my mother by adoption, Greta (Max) Cohen; my grandparents Fanny and Julius Gerstl, and my oldest brother by adoption, Ed Cohen; my rescuers from genocide, Frantz and Mine Vandenheuvel. This book is also dedicated to everyone who has mentored me and cared about me – and to everyone who strives to build a world filled with social, economic, and political justice.

1

POWER, IDEOLOGY, AND SOCIAL SERVICES

Treat the earth well: it was not given to you by your parents,
it was loaned to you by your children. We do not inherit the
Earth from our Ancestors, we borrow it from our Children.
— An ancient Indigenous teaching

The loud chirping of birds woke me up. It was early May
2008 in Tyendinaga, a First Nations reserve on territory of
the Mohawks of the Bay of Quinte in Southeast Ontario. I
was at a culture camp that included twenty-nine Indigenous students. This culture camp was part of a social work educational program organized by the First Nations Technical Institute in partnership with Toronto's Ryerson University.

We had agreed that for the week of culture camp we would live
on the land. This was not a particularly rugged culture camp. We
were in a public park, we had brought our own tents, and we had
access to running water and electricity. We had applied for and
received government funding to hire Indigenous traditional teachers.
The funds also allowed us to hire First Nations cooks, who jovially
prepared our meals from a kitchen inside their camp trailer. When
morning came we could eagerly head to the picnic tables placed
inside a large white tent where we lined up for hot coffee, tea, and
breakfast.

Culture camp was the second part of a social work course I was
co-teaching with Banakonda Kennedy-Kish (Bell), a traditional practitioner from the Anishinaabe Nation who had accumulated deep

1

knowledge about First Nations culture. Students in this program came from different communities in Ontario that included Haudenosaunee, Anishinaabe, and Cree nations. They were taking these university courses on a part-time basis, and most of them were employed full-time in a variety of social services within their communities. This off-campus program had some key objectives: to provide access to university education for Indigenous people, who had historically been excluded from post-secondary institutions; to foster favourable self-images related to the students' Indigenous identities; and to strengthen student capacities to provide respectful and effective social services to their own communities.

While some students in this group were already quite knowledgeable about their own culture, others had been so assimilated that they had little such knowledge. At the camp traditional teachers provided cultural explanations about protecting water and about lighting a sacred fire that would become a focal point for our outdoor learning-teaching sessions. We heard magnificent Iroquoian teachings about "The Peacemakers Journey" and "The Good Mind." In addition, with instruction and hands-on assistance, each of us made either a hand drum or a water drum. We fasted for a day on the land to gain an appreciation of the linkages between Creation, spirituality, and nature's gifts. We learned Haudenosaunee songs and dances. During culture camp I was mainly a listener-participant, which allowed me to deepen my understanding of Indigenous culture and its wisdom regarding how to be good helpers to individuals, families, and communities.

Later, Professor Lynn Lavallée, who is Métis of Algonquin, Cree, and French heritage, carried out a formal evaluation of the culture camp. Using Indigenous research methods (Lavallée 2009a; Hart 2009a; Wilson 2008) that included cultural protocols and sharing circles, Lavallée reported that students experienced culture camp as "exciting" "enjoyable," "very nurturing," and "an awesome learning experience." These favourable responses reflect the exhilaration that students experienced in affirming their cultural identify. As one student put it:

For the longest time we have been denied our ability to be Native and only in this generation are we starting to pick it back up. And what we are picking up are resemblances amongst our traditions, our languages and our cultures. It's coming back. Coming to this group, each one of us from a different tradition – Cree, Ojibwe, Anishnaabe, Haudenosaunee or whomever – if we were to each build our own separate ladders it would take a long time for them to be built but if we took pieces from each of us it would be built a lot faster. And it doesn't matter whose piece of the ladder we use, the point is we will get out together. For me, that is what culture camp is about. (Lavallée 2009b: 14–15)

This breaking out of the silence imposed by colonialism, and not doing it alone but as part of a group, generated a sense of solidarity to move out of an oppressive past. Such solidarity is being supported by developments across the country through a resurgence of cultural traditions that had been suppressed but are now being celebrated through Indigenous art, language, and ceremonies (Porter 2010). After analyzing her data, Lavallée concluded, "Students felt that this traditional learning was extremely important in their current and future roles as helpers in their communities" (17). These future roles may well include a political path that leads to the mobilization of more Indigenous voices calling upon Canadians to correct historical injustices.

A little over a month after the culture camp, Canada's residential schools and their flagrant violations of human rights received national attention. At a special gathering of the Canadian House of Commons, on June 4, Prime Minister Stephen Harper made a public apology:

The government of Canada built an educational system in which very young children were often forcibly removed from their homes and often taken far from their communities. Many were inadequately fed, clothed and housed. . . . First Nations, Inuit and Métis languages and cultural practices were prohibited in these schools. Tragically, some of these children died while attending residential schools and others never returned home. . . . On behalf of the Government of Canada and all Canadians, I . . . apologize to aboriginal peoples for Canada's role in the Indian residential school system. . . . The burden of this experience has been on your shoulders for far too long. The burden is properly ours as a government, and as a country. (House of Commons 2008)

After this apology, Indigenous leaders who had been invited to the House of Commons were given the opportunity to respond. Phil Fontaine, National Chief of the Assembly of First Nations, stated:

> This morning our elders held a condolence ceremony for those who never heard an apology, never received compensation, yet courageously fought assimilation so that we could witness this day. Together, we remember and honour them for it was they who suffered the most as they witnessed generation after generation of their children taken from their families' love and guidance. . . . Brave survivors, through the telling of their painful stories, have stripped white supremacy of its authority and legitimacy.

Mary Simon, president of the Inuit Tapiriit Kanatami, offered a sense of caution:

> Let us not be lulled into an impression that when the sun rises tomorrow morning, the pain and scars will miraculously be gone. They will not. But a new day has dawned, a new day heralded by a commitment to reconciliation and building a new relationship with Inuit, Métis and First Nations.

Similarly, Clem Chartier, president of the Métis National Council, suggested that the work to be done was by no means finished:

> The Prime Minister and the Minister of Indian Affairs know that although I am very sincere and happy, perhaps, that this is happening, I also feel deeply conflicted, because there is still misunderstanding about the situation of the Métis Nation, our history and our contemporary situation. . . . I am one of the survivors of a Métis residential school. . . . The Métis Nation of western Canada, which has been excluded from many things by the workings of this House and its policies, wants in.

Beverly Jacobs, president of the Native Women's Association of Canada, added:

> Prior to the residential schools system, prior to colonization, the women in our communities were very well respected and honoured for the role that they have in our communities as being the life givers, being the caretakers of the spirit that we bring to mother earth. We have been given those responsibilities to look after our children and to bring that spirit into this physical world. Residential schools caused so much harm to that respect and to that honour. . . . Now it is about our responsibilities today, the decisions that we make today and how they will affect seven generations from now. . . . What is it that this government is going to do in the future to help our people? (House of Commons 2008)

When reporters asked Aboriginal peoples across the country about their reaction to this public apology, the responses were mixed. They ranged from "To have a government today say, finally, yes, something was horribly wrong to treat us as less than human. . . . I needed that" to "Residential school wrecked my life and an apology won't fix it" (Strojeck 2008: A17). This was the first time that the Government of Canada had made such a public, unconditional apology to Canada's Indigenous communities. While the federal government has yet to match this apology with effective action to address the intergenerational consequences of residential schools, the apology is nevertheless an important benchmark in the uphill process of obtaining justice.

Significantly, the apology's focus was restricted to the harm caused by the policies of enforced assimilation. The Prime Minister was silent about genocide – that is, the killing of Indigenous people by British and French colonial powers who set about to destroy Indigenous communities and culture to clear the way for the massive theft of Indigenous land by European settlers. The Prime Minister was also silent about the violation of colonial treaties with Indigenous Nations. He did not refer to the ways in which colonialism and militarism had produced unjust enrichment flowing into the coffers of business and government elites in Canada, England, and France. He said nothing about the flip side of this wealth transfer: the destruction and unjust impoverishment of Indigenous communities in Canada, with results that are still reverberating today, as evidenced by the tragically high rates of suicide, imprisonment, and poverty among Aboriginal peoples.

Today, business corporations, local and international, after some token consultations with the affected communities, continue to do business as usual in planning and implementing the extraction of timber, mining, oil, water, and other parts of nature from traditional Indigenous territories. We clearly have a long way to go before Canada can hold its head high in its relationship with Inuit, Métis, and First Nations peoples.

At the same time, people within mainstream Canadian society also experience different types of oppression. The steady trend towards greater and greater inequality between rich and poor is another example of harm being done to innocent people. While some people might question whether this gap is indeed harmful, there is little dispute about the reality that the gap is substantial (Curry-Stevens 2009: 42–43). Statistics Canada researchers René Morissette and Xuelin Zhang (2006) calculated the extent of concentration of Canadian wealth during the period of 1984 to 2004. They found that "the top 10% of families came to own 56% of Canadians' net worth in 1999, and 58% in 2005. . . . Average wealth did not improve for the families in the bottom fifth of the distributions. In contrast, it rose about $19,000 in the middle group and more than $400,000 in the top fifth." Unless there is a strong public outcry, this wealth gap will continue to sow ever deeper division among Canadians.

A similar process is happening globally. Numerous studies have documented the gap on the international level. As just one example, a project carried out under the auspices of the World Institute for Development (2008) at the United Nations University in Helsinki found: "The wealth share estimates reveal that the richest 2% of adult individuals own more than half of all global wealth. In contrast the bottom half of wealth holders together hold barely 1% of global wealth" (Davies et al. 2008: 7).

At the same time some people might ask: Are these growing inequalities really harmful? After all, don't we have charities, social services, and social programs to assist the disadvantaged? Canada's federal government, along with the national associations of social work educators and practitioners, conducted an extensive study to find out what was happening in the social services sector.* Researchers surveyed 109 social service employers and carried out over three hundred in-depth interviews of social service managers, educators, and employees. The study's findings, reported in 2001, stated: "Increased workloads, having to do more with less, and service users who are experiencing more intense, multi-dimensional challenges to their social, psychological and economic survival – all contribute significantly to making social service employment extremely demanding and sometimes very dispiriting" (Stephenson et al. 2001: 2).

Some ten years after the publication of this report, the situation continues to deteriorate. Social justice activists see direct links between the deterioration of social services, the growth of indifference towards the poor, and the expansion of inequalities in Canada. But are these trends really so bad?

The answers vary because in the first place there are sharply opposing opinions about the sources and consequences of inequalities. These disagreements seem to have less to do with a recognition of "hard facts" and more to do with personal values, attitudes, and views about what is fair. Some people argue that social and economic success is built on different talents, on hard work, and on a willingness to take risks. From this position, they take a giant leap and suggest that inequalities between rich and poor are caused entirely by personal choices. In other words, any one person can become financially successful by choosing to be enterprising, working very hard, and simply having talent.

According to this social construction of "choice," if individual people choose to be lazy or refuse to work at all, they will be poor. Poverty, therefore, is a simple matter of choice – and if people live in poverty, too bad, because "they choose it through their irresponsible behaviour." Therefore, so the argument goes, social services must be

---

* The terms "social agencies" and "social services" are often used interchangeably. Social agencies and social services are organizations that employ social service providers to deliver programs to people who are called "service users" or "consumers" or "clients." Social service providers may be social workers or, more generally, social service workers.

minimal. "Why should we help people, when their poverty is their own fault?" This way of understanding poverty and inequality is part of a conservative ideology that extols great wealth as a condition brought about entirely through a person's own merits. Sometimes called *meritocracy*, this view justifies huge inequalities as a fair outcome of conditions deemed to be based on either wonderful private achievements or dismal personal failures. In this approach, well-being hinges entirely upon individual efforts and making the right choices. This line of thought is also known as *individualism*.

Colleen Lundy, former director of the School of Social Work at Carleton University, points out that social workers, like others, are influenced by attitudes linked to assumptions and beliefs:

> Social attitudes based on their gender, race/ethnicity, class, sexual orientation, and the problems with which they are struggling are often influenced by ideology – ideology which is embedded in the policies and practices of social institutions. For example, the act of placing the full responsibility/blame on individuals for their circumstances is rooted in a particular ideology or set of ideas and beliefs. (2004: 51–52)

Conservative ideology assumes that everyone has the same choice and therefore everyone has to accept the consequences of the choices they make. Furthermore, government should not interfere with these outcomes. Indeed, conservative ideology claims that the "best government is the least government" – a government that allows individuals to remain in charge of their own destinies so long as they don't interfere with the same rights of others. According to this theory of individualism, the incentive to succeed and excel is a positive force that fuels our economy and instructs us how best to avoid poverty (see Swift et al. 2003; Bailey and Gayle 2003).

By contrast, people who challenge the growth of inequalities begin with values of equity and inclusion. In contrast to conservative ideology, we believe that the huge financial rewards received by the members of small elites have little or nothing to do with their individual merit – but a lot to do with the existence of privilege. We see those who defend inequality as doing their best to hide the full story about why some people have power over others. In our view, it is not power itself that is problematic. After all, parents have been granted legitimate power over their young children, and social services are sometimes called in when this power is abused. Similarly, teachers have legitimate power over young students; again, if this power is abused, the educational institution or justice system may become involved. A different danger stems from power when it is illegitimate – power that, when exercised, reinforces the condition of illegitimate privilege possessed by one group of people who abuse the well-being of others.

I use the term "privilege" to refer to benefits that are received by one group at the expense of another group due to the way in which economic and political power is organized in society. For example, in the days when women did not have the right to vote, that condition was the result of power being organized in such a way that only men had the advantage of voting. Voting was seen as a right that men had, but more accurately it was a privilege held only by men. At the time, it was seen as "normal" for men to have this advantage – and it remained so until the condition was challenged by women. While this privilege was real, it was not legitimate because it allowed males to exclude women from political power. This privilege in turn reinforced the unjust power of males over women in many other spheres of life.

In a similar way today economic and political power in our society is still organized in ways that allocate advantages to some people at the expense of others. The consequent injustices are often not recognized because these unequal power relationships are still often seen by many people as "normal." To achieve social justice we need to expose and de-legitimate these unjust power inequalities. It is not only the privilege that is illegitimate, but also the unjust power that channels advantages for some at the expense of others.

At the same time, the word "privilege" is often used in our culture to refer to highly desirable situations – we say, for instance, "It is a privilege to know you." For that reason I use the terms "illegitimate privilege" and "unjust privilege" to alert readers to the harmful, divisive, and oppressive sense of the term. Another reason for using the term "illegitimate privilege" is because conservative ideology tries to convince us that the privileged have earned their greater power and status; and therefore our economic system must not be questioned. By deconstructing the term "privilege," we can gain a fresh understanding of how inequalities are caused and justified. As Bob Mullaly observes: "The flip side of the coin of oppression is privilege. . . . If we want to truly understand oppression, we must understand privilege. Oppression and privilege go hand in hand" (2010: 287).

In 2008, when the economic collapse began in the United States, it quickly expanded globally into the worst financial disaster since the Great Depression of the 1930s. Suddenly, the cheerleaders for conservative ideology found themselves on the defensive. There is a particular irony in witnessing CEOs and other business leaders falling over themselves in asking for generous assistance from government funds to shore up their sagging corporate fortunes, when not long before these same business leaders, true to their conservative ideology, were urging governments to restrict or eliminate government welfare payments to people living in poverty.

For the moment at least, conservative ideology is in trouble. There is a growing public understanding about the issues that political conservatives ignore: the contradictions and serious double standards related to how economic production, policies, laws, institutions, and narratives establish privilege for some people (extensive education, business or employment connections, large inheritances) while creating huge barriers for others (racism, or frail health due to childhood poverty). In short, the structures of our society favour some people and punish others (McKenzie 2010; Grossman 2010). These imbalances are called *systemic inequalities* because they are created by society's structures, also known as the "system" within which we live.

Conservatives do not see, much less recognize, these systemic injustices. Most often, if they are among the elite class, it is because they benefit from these injustices. Who are these elites? They tend to be rich, White, heterosexual, able-bodied, non-Indigenous males. By contrast, the people who have doors slammed in their faces tend to be Indigenous people, Afro-Canadians, Hispanics, and other racialized groups, or lesbians, gays, bisexual, transgender, and intersex people, or unemployed or underemployed young adults – and a dis-proportion number of them are women and people with disabilities. Many of these people also work very hard, often at more than one job. Yet they can barely make ends meet, or, indeed, they live in poverty. Some people among the affluent class also work very hard, but the excessive financial rewards they gain from doing so are totally out of proportion to their effort and talents.

Unequal opportunities or biased outcomes are only part of the picture. Another part is the way in which inequalities are aggravated by the pressure groups of rich elites that influence government poli-cies. In one study John McMurtry points out how affluent people have influenced our tax system, which he calls a war of the rich against the poor; and, he says, it is a war "waged at all levels of the tax system. Ever more tax evasion, offshore banking, tax loopholes, transfer pricing and corporate shell companies combine with ever lower upfront tax rates for the wealthy and big business and extrava-gant tax and other subsidies to transnational oil corporations, factory agribusiness, weapons manufacturers" (2009: 1).

Tax cuts and tax evasion mean less revenue collected, which translates into cuts in public services, including cuts in social pro-grams. People who go to social services seeking assistance are likely to encounter less help and more bureaucratic hurdles. Yet it is pre-cisely when greater levels of poverty and inequalities exist in a soci-ety that there are greater needs for additional social services capable of providing effective help.

Writer Ruth Latta reports (2009: 17) on a study by two British epidemiologists, Richard Wilkinson and Kate Pickett, who looked at wealth patterns in the world's twenty richest countries. They found that social problems "are related to the distribution of wealth in a society, not to its overall wealth." These researchers conclude: "The bigger the income gap, the worse the rates of mental illness, sub-stance abuse, teen pregnancy, male violence, homicide, incarcera-tion, and short life expectancy." In other words, larger inequalities lead to larger social problems.

In light of these damning results from countries with steadfast inequalities, it is not surprising that those of us committed to equity find that a progressive, rather than conservative, ideology is a better guide to the dismantling of unfair advantages and barriers. Mullaly suggests: "Developing an understanding of what privilege and oppression are and how they operate and how we participate in them is the first step in working for change" (2010: 313).

My aim in this book, similarly, is to first of all focus on privilege and to validate what people are saying about their own experiences of oppression. This means, for example, that non-Aboriginal people like me need to open ourselves to examining our own colonial privilege at the same time as we are learning about the lived experiences of Aboriginal people – as reflected by the students in our culture camp. These types of "tuning in" processes – focusing on ourselves as well as on a wide diversity of groups that have been disadvantaged in numerous ways – are important steps along the road of helping people to achieve their dignity.

My intention is to join with the many other voices who are calling for the dismantling of all oppressions. I believe that when enough people say "no more" to harmful practices – when we agree that the case is critical for action – then conditions will be ripe for a transformation from oppression to well-being.

2 NAMING AND RESISTING INJUSTICES

> The earth has enough for the needs of all, but not for the greed of the few.
> — Mahatma Gandhi

First the bad news: the scope, quantity, and areas of injustices, both in Canada and internationally, have deep roots. They are extensive, and therefore not easily dislodged. Some people reap handsome benefit from injustice, and usually work hard to protect, enlarge, and entrench their well-established privilege. They will also try to ridicule, marginalize, intimidate, and silence individuals, networks, and organizations that expose this unfair privilege. A review of these injustices can be discouraging because we can sense the despair and hopelessness experienced by people who find themselves trapped in oppressive conditions through no fault of their own.

Now the good news: these injustices are being challenged in many ways, and victories have been won in the campaign for greater equity in our society. Many people on their own, or as part of networks and organizations, have concluded that equity, inclusion, and democratic accountability are not only possible and desirable, but also critically urgent. These equity-seekers, both inside and outside of social services, are joining together to learn and to educate others. They are advocating, organizing, demonstrating, and mobilizing public support for greater social justice. Part of this process is the discovery and naming of various sets of privilege.

COLONIAL PRIVILEGE

Colonialism has been with us for a long time. Both in the past and continuing today the need for the denial of colonial privilege has been extremely strong and, in light of the atrocities associated with colonialism, understandable. For hundreds of years England, France, Spain, Portugal, and other European nations used a combination of force, gunboat diplomacy, and trade to exploit the people, lands, and natural resources of other continents. When I was a public-school student in Ottawa our classroom walls had large world maps mounted on them showing the British Empire coloured pink across large chunks of different parts of the Earth. I was taught about colonization in benign terms: that the "voyages of discovery" had brought European cultures and civilized values to the rest of the world. Only much later did I realize that "discovery" really meant conquest, frequently accompanied by blood-soaked legacies of slavery and genocide. Ramesh Thakur, senior vice-rector of the United Nations University in Tokyo, puts it this way: "They came to deliver us from local tyrants and stayed to rule as foreign despots. In the name of enlightenment, they defiled our lands, plundered our resources and expanded their empires" (2004: A21).

As a White person I found it extremely disturbing to learn how Whites had considered themselves so "superior" that they had forcibly imposed their religions, economies, and racism upon people around the world – and that included the First Nations in what came to be called Canada. This oppression has been well documented (Royal Commission on Aboriginal Peoples 1996; Sinclair 2009a; Strega and Sohki Aski Esquao 2009). For example, a report issued by the B.C. provincial government states:

> Europeans did not only bring cultural chauvinism to North America. They also brought concepts of land use and ownership that thinly veiled the most systematic theft of land in the history of human existence. Because Europeans had a view of Nature as a thing to be brought under human control, lands that were not so dominated were considered unused. Coupled with that view was the concept of private land ownership. Consequently, "undeveloped" land was unused land

and unused land was unowned land. Based on this cultural justification, Europeans were to engage in, and condone, a violation of their
own international laws regarding the relations between nations. They
confiscated virtually all the territories of the Aboriginal Nations of
North America. (Aboriginal Committee, Community Panel 1992: 14)

Michael Anthony Hart (Kaskitémahikan) from the Fisher River Cree
Nation in Southern Manitoba points out (2009b: 26–27) that colonialism continues today in Canada. It is "driven by a worldview and
processes that embrace dominion, self-righteousness and greed, and
affects all levels of Indigenous peoples' lives – the national, communal, familial and individual – and insidiously interferes with all
aspects of Indigenous peoples' lives, including their spiritual practices, emotional wellbeing, physical health and knowledge."

The initial beneficiaries of colonialism were European settlers
and traders who gained immense privileges to enrich themselves
financially. Though guilty of crimes against humanity, at the time they
received the backing of the commercial, political, legal, and religious
leadership in England and France. Consequently, these leaders provided a moral veneer of respectability to justify not only the colonization of North America, but also the enslavement of Africans whose
forced labour was exploited in the United States and Canada. Just as
colonial leaders insulted and labelled slaves "subhuman, " to justify
treating human beings as commodities, similar insults were inflicted
upon the First Nations to justify attempts to crush their civilization.

Although the crimes against Indigenous children in residential
schools across Canada have become relatively well-known, less well-
known are the ways in which social workers have harmed Indigenous peoples. For example, what has been called the "Sixties Scoop"
refers to the widespread practice, starting during the 1960s, of social
workers forcibly removing Aboriginal children from their families
and sending them to non-Aboriginal foster homes and group homes
or out for adoption, all with the approval of the courts. The foster
parents or adoptive parents were mostly indifferent or hostile to
Indigenous culture.

University of Regina professor Raven Sinclair (Ótiskewápíwskew), who is Cree/Assinniboine and Saulteaux from Gordon's and

Kawacatoose First Nations, researched the "Sixties Scoop." Sinclair notes that even today Aboriginal children are still being swept into the child welfare system in disproportionately high numbers (2009b: 94). She has also found that researchers and practitioners who focus on Aboriginal children raised in non-Aboriginal homes tend to emphasize the loss of cultural identity as a primary theme. In challenging that approach, Sinclair states:

> From the stories, narratives and testimonials of adoptees, many Aboriginal adoptees have struggled greatly to "fit" into White society outside of their family context. . . . The problem with viewing identity as the issue is that the focus of the problem then rests with the child. The literature thus states that adolescents "no longer fit" rather than "a racialized society does not allow them to fit." (104)

Instead of pathologizing Aboriginal adoptees for their alleged cultural deficits, Sinclair reframes the issue as racism: "Adolescent behavioural problems, adoption breakdowns and adult psychological turmoil are linked, in adoptees' testimonials, to the intra- and extra-familial racism and abuse experienced by adoptees and the emotional fall-out from those experiences of racism" (107).

In this regard systemic racism has clearly had an impact on child welfare services, but it has also made itself felt within social services generally. Professor Bonnie Freeman, an Algonquin and Mohawk, Bear Clan, from the Six Nations of the Grand River Territory, states:

> When Aboriginal people go into drug and alcohol treatment programs, for example, many of these interventions do not incorporate an understanding of Indigenous history, cultural values, beliefs, and social dynamics. Without a historical understanding of the generations of trauma and grief, practitioners cannot address the underlying issues of shame, lack of identify and belonging that stem from continued oppression and marginalization over generations. (2007: 103)

Despite the waves of assimilationist practices, Aboriginal communities struggled as best they could to retain their distinct cultures and values. This history of resistance has contributed to changes for the better – residential schools, for example, no longer exist – but the intergenerational impact of these destructive institutions continues to reverberate through Indigenous communities. Nevertheless, community members are engaged in an intensive revitalization of their cultural traditions, ceremonies, and spirituality. The cultural rebirth is happening not only at grassroots and community levels but also through Indigenous political organizations at the local, regional, and national levels. The revival is accompanied by government negotiations to transfer services, including social services, to Aboriginal communities.

Still, although members of Aboriginal communities have the knowledge and ability to deliver the services, the experience of taking over the programs has proved "frustrating." As Malcolm Saulis, an Aboriginal social work educator from the Maliseet nation in the Maritimes, points out, the communities still do not have the autonomy needed to carry out "programming in a way that fully takes into account the culture of their people." While Aboriginal communities might spend a great deal of time learning how "to conceptualize more culturally appropriate models of program or policy delivery," Saulis says (2006: 116): "The bureaucrats they work with in various government departments have not engaged in such rigorous conceptual thinking. . . . Most policy directions articulated by governments hint at the possibility of meeting the cultural needs of Aboriginal populations, but in practice the bureaucratic mindset prevails."

Saulis notes that some government officials are recognizing that imposing a mainstream view has prevented the development of effective Aboriginal social services, and that a paradigm shift is needed that would allow for the expression of an Aboriginal world view within Aboriginal social welfare programs. Aboriginal "governance, cultural and traditional practices, and social organization" need to be an integral part of those programs – although "a major obstacle in implementing the new paradigm has been the scarcity of funds" (119).

Despite severe funding shortages, some social service success stories have still managed to come forward. Calvin Morrisseau, for instance, has chronicled his personal healing journey. His life as a youth in the Anishinaabe community was filled with the violent consequences of alcoholism, which he witnessed in both his family and his community. From the age of twelve, he too become addicted to alcohol as a way of escaping the painful anguish of rejection, confusion, and loneliness. After hitting rock bottom, and considering suicide, he struggled to turn his life around. Help came when Morrisseau went to his community's Elders and found a form of alcohol treatment framed within his Anishinaabe culture:

> While in treatment, I was given some tools that would help me stay clean and sober. I began to get in touch with the wounded child inside and I began to tell his story. The shame I felt began to dissipate. I began to see myself in a different light. I began to know and respect myself. (Morrisseau 1999: 99–100)

His healing journey became a model for others who wanted to pull themselves out of a downward spiral of despair. He subsequently became a program manager for an Indigenous social service to help others both counteract the intergenerational impact of residential schools and address oppressive social conditions. For, as one group of researchers put it: "Extremely high poverty and unemployment rates, critical housing shortages, and a lack of human and fiscal resources to meet basic service needs of Aboriginal people characterize the current fiscal and economic environment for most Aboriginal people" (Stephenson et al. 2001: 186; see also Wilson and Macdonald 2010).

As I thought about Morrisseau's experience with colonialism, I became more aware that the colonial privileges I possess tend to be invisible. Like others whose families have immigrated to Canada within the past centuries, I usually do not see that, along with my immediate circles of family, friends, and colleagues, I gain benefits from an infrastructure of institutions located in towns and cities and on land that is available to me only because of the violent displacement of the original inhabitants. As authors Tim Schouls, John Olthuis, and Diane Engelstad remind us, "All non-native Canadians have benefited tremendously from racist policies, from theft of land and from defaults on solemn treaties" (1992:14). Colonial oppression does not stand alone. As we become more aware of colonial privilege, we also learn about its links to other systemic violations, such as racism.

Racialized Privilege

For U.S. anti-racist educator Peggy McIntosh, a key personal lesson about racism was what she was taught not to see: "As a White person, I realized I had been taught about racism as something which puts others at a disadvantage, but I had been taught not to see one of its corollary aspects, white privilege, which puts me at an advantage." Her writing had a major impact on anti-racist education. She suggested that each White person write out a list of the privileges they experience based on their whiteness. The purpose is to identify privileges in "taken for granted" areas and move them into our critical consciousness. She gives examples of her invisible privilege: "I can be sure that if I need legal or medical help, my race will not work against me," and "I am never asked to speak for all the people of my racial group" (1998: 147–50; McIntosh 2007). McIntosh's list includes noticing that her whiteness is not only well represented in history books but is also prominent among people favourably portrayed by the media. The purpose is not to create guilt about whiteness, but rather to clarify a hurtful or damaging condition and then work towards changing it.

Yet it is tempting to evade one's own collusion with racism. Social service directors typically become indignant when critics suggest that they are implicated in what amounts to racist practices. Their indignation implies that they view racism as being restricted to the intentional conduct of bigots. In their book *Colour of Democracy: Racism in Canadian Society*, Frances Henry and Carol Tator differentiate three categories of racism: individual, institutional-systemic, and cultural-ideological (2006: 51–53). They describe individual racism as attitudes and everyday behaviour based on beliefs about the superiority of the person's own racial group, and about the inferiority of other groups. Individual racism is usually deliberate and expresses itself in glances, gestures, forms of speech, and physical movements.

> Sometimes it is not even consciously experienced by its perpetrators, but it is immediately and painfully felt by its victims – the empty seat next to a person of colour, which is the last to be occupied in a

crowded bus; the slight movement away from a person of colour in an elevator; the over-attention to the Black customer in the shop; the inability to make direct eye contact with a person of colour. (54)

By contrast, institutional racism expresses itself in an institution's policies, practices, and procedures that create advantage or privilege for certain racialized people. At this institutional level, racism does not have to be intentional. Rather, it is the outcome of exclusion – in, for example, hiring practices – that makes the behaviour racist. Sometimes the institutional form is called systemic racism, which is when the laws, rules, and norms woven into society "result in an unequal distribution of economic, political and social resources and rewards among various racial groups" (53). The reality that Canada's political and economic elites are still primarily White, while the general population is mixed in colour, is an example of systemic racism.

Cultural and ideological racism consist of overarching cultural symbols that reinforce both individual and institutional forms of racism. These symbols include ideas and values expressed through language, religion, and art, and are deeply woven – for example, by the mass media and the arts – into the fabric of mainstream culture (Henry and Tator: 2006: 53). For example, the word "black" tends to be associated with something bad, such as "blackmail," "black sheep," and "blacklisted," while the idea of "white" tends to be associated with being clean and pure. Another example is the prevailing understanding that Christopher Columbus "discovered" America – an understanding that prepares our minds for a lost continent and therefore a "lost" people in need of "redemption."

Henry and her co-authors point out that racism is a social construction of difference and serves to reproduce existing power relationships. Similar to colonialism, racism in Canada causes whiteness to remain largely invisible as the "normal" reference point for judging different ethno-racialized groups (Henry and Tator 2006: 53; Yee and Dumbrill 2002: 103).

In addition to the abusive treatment of Indigenous people and Afro-Canadians, which began centuries ago, later examples of racism in Canada include the exploitation of Chinese railway workers, the mistreatment of Japanese Canadians during the Second World War, and the denial of immigration to Jews seeking refuge from Nazi regimes, to name a few. Current examples include racial profiling by police departments and a rising number of racist incidents against members of Moslem and Jewish communities (Honderich 2003: A27; Zijad 2010; League for Human Rights of B'nai Brith 2009).

Given that racism pervades all of the country's institutions, including its social services, challenging it, as social work author and educator Steven Hick notes, "demands that social work practitioners work to change their own awareness and practices." But, he adds, they also need to change "the practice of those around them, institutional policies and procedures, and social relations and systems that operate, both overtly and covertly, to perpetuate racism" (2006: 244). The task is daunting. Not much has changed in the years since anti-racist social work educators Narda Razack and Donna Jeffery pointed out, "There is little evidence that the social work profession has attended to its own complicity in reproducing racialized systems of domination" (2002: 263).

Anti-racist education is intended to make social service providers, and others as well, more aware of both the hidden and not-so-hidden dynamics of racism so that we can work for change. But staff development costs money, which is in extremely short supply within social services. Not only are funds practically non-existent for anti-racist education, but also, when it comes to combatting other prejudices such as those based on gender, class, sexuality, age, or disabilities, the funds are practically non-existent. Extreme shortages of funds are typical today for most public-sector services, ranging from health to education, but in social services cuts have been so severe that even basic service delivery has been compromised.

Class Privilege

In 2003 the Canadian Association of Social Workers published the results of a survey of over nine hundred child protection workers across the country. The survey found that service providers had such large caseloads that they had no time for relationship-based work: "This group of front line practitioners universally identified the fact that they are unable to get to know their clients, that they cannot spend quality time with children and families, as the most significant impediment to their ability to do good practice" (Herbert 2003:10).

The large unwieldy caseloads are the result of underfunding, and they are typical of many social service agencies today. From 1996 to 2004 a cumulative total of almost $250 billion in government revenue became unavailable due to federal and provincial tax cuts (Yalnizyan and Pascal 2004: 11–12). The results were substantial cutbacks in all government services in Canada, including social services. These cuts are closely connected to yet another set of privileges, this time based on social class.

Even though some Canadians live opulent lifestyles while others barely eke out a living, there is a huge sense of denial about the existence of class stratification in our society. This denial creates the illusion of equity – fostered by a conservative ideology that seems embarrassed by the substantial class differences created by our economic system. Similar to the invisibility of privilege derived from colonialism and racism, the consequences of class privilege are often seen as "natural," or are hidden from view. Indeed, rich elites have developed elaborate ways of expanding their class privileges and hiding the harmful consequences of their actions. The rich, for instance, benefit from the largely hidden privilege of an undue and undemocratic influence over the direction of Canadian society. Their special interest groups are the most powerful in the country – from the Canadian Chamber of Commerce and Canadian Manufacturers and Exporters to the C.D. Howe Institute and Fraser Institute and a host of other business and right-wing political lobbies. Their messages are further amplified by a repeated chorus of editorials from media outlets, almost all of them managed and owned by wealthy individuals or corporations.

The Canadian Council of Chief Executives, for instance, represents 150 of Canada's biggest corporations, with assets totalling over $4.5 trillion (Canadian Council of Chief Executives 2010). With its relatively easy access to top public officials, this Council argues, again and again, "Responsible and carefully timed reductions to both corporate and personal income tax rates are essential" (Canadian

Council of Chief Executives 2009). But this claim about what is "essential" raises the question: "Essential for whom?" While this CEO Council argues that lower taxes are essential for all Canadians, the claim does not hold up to close scrutiny. Comparative studies by economists and other experts have shown that Western European countries, which have higher taxes than Canada does, have economies that are just as healthy if not more so than ours (Lee 2004). One study concludes: "It is well known that taxes and transfers reduce productivity. Well known – but unsupported by statistics and history" (Lindert 2004: 1). For the companies, of course, lower taxation means higher profits.

Truly, these special interests are getting the tax cuts they want, and feel they need. But who elected them to be our spokespersons? When they say "we know what Canada needs," who did they ask, apart from economists on their payroll and other highly privileged CEOs? Yet in the end, what these big-business pressure groups have asked for has been delivered by governments: significant tax cuts for corporations and for the wealthy.

Contrary to the glowing promises made by the Canadian Council of Chief Executives about the benefits of lower taxes, tax cuts – in combination with other unfair taxation policies – have had a devastating impact on Canadian well-being. Tax cuts have caused a significant deterioration in our public health, public education, public libraries, and other public services. Tax cuts have also resulted in deep setbacks for the delivery of social services, with especially devastating effects on people living in poverty. With big holes in what used to be the social safety net, more and more people are homeless or near-homeless (Shapcott 2009).

Economics commentator Hugh Mackenzie (2007) reviewed the Canadian statistics on the growing rich-poor gap, and after analyzing who benefits the most from tax cuts, he concluded: "Our provincial and federal governments have been talking tax cuts [for everyone], but those cuts went into the pockets of the richest of the rich. And that tax break only bolstered the unprecedented growth in the share of income going to Canada's richest." Something is terribly wrong when government policies, such as tax cuts, result in substantial benefits for the rich and privileged few in society, while the same policies cause a great many others to lose the benefit of a variety of public services – and the steepest loss is experienced, again and again, by the poorest of the poor. These outcomes make a mockery of a democracy that is supposed to serve all people, not just the privileged. These outcomes, driven by a wealthy class, by large private corporations, and by their spokespersons, offer conclusive evidence that while Canada still has the outer, superficial shell of democracy, its inner substance has been secreted out, captured by the privileged class and their corporations.

The vested interests are clear enough. Economist Armine Yalnizyan notes:

> In 1998 the average (annual) compensation of Canada's top 100 CEOs was $3.5 million. By 2007 it had tripled to $10.4 million. During the same period, the average wage of full-time workers increased from $33,000 to $40,000 – an increase that was just a little less than the inflation of prices (22.7%) over these years. . . . The average pay of the top 100 CEOs went from 104 times that of the average full-time worker to 259 times. (2009: 15–16)

Despite a rash of high-profile corporate scandals, large corporations remain credible institutions, in no small measure because their commercials, newspapers, TV networks, and magazines all deliver the same message: big corporations create jobs, supply what we need, and pay taxes. Many years ago the Italian activist and thinker Antonio Gramsci, writing in his *Prison Notebooks*, had a word for this dynamic process: *hegemony*, a condition achieved when we acquiesce to the power of dominant groups in society because their power is accepted as "natural." In a brief outline of Gramsci's thought, Peter Steven notes that the concept of hegemony refers to "a form of power or rule not limited to direct political control but one where those who have power maintain their position through the creation of a particular world view, one that seems to be based on common sense" (2004: 52–53).

This "common sense" has camouflaged much of the injustices produced by capitalist privileges. Not that top-down, communist regimes provide an attractive alternative. During the twentieth century these centrally planned and controlled state economies proved disastrous both for human rights and environmental integrity. Under the promise of equality, top-heavy state bureaucracies from Eastern Europe and the Soviet Union to China used police and military forces to suppress their own citizens.

But have the globalized corporate bureaucracies of the West found any better answers? Their excessive wealth accumulation and rapacious stock-market speculation, obscene economic disparities, environmental decay, and narrow electoral choices all demonstrate the abysmal record of organizing global institutions upon the cracked foundation of private greed. Contributing to gross corporate irresponsibility have been the so-called free-trade agreements that encourage global corporations to shop around for nations that offer the most favourable working conditions – which means the most oppressive – and sometimes, too, where labour union leaders are assassinated and where governments are willing to slash taxes and ignore environmental protection. Supporting this entrenchment of global corporate privileges have been the World Bank and the International Monetary Fund. These institutions have established global financial procedures that insist upon unjustly harsh conditions for loans and credits to poor nations. These processes have violated human rights, as well as cut social programs, sold off public resources, and removed food subsidies (Lundy: 2004: 10).

An eloquent voice for a more authentic democracy comes from one of India's leading physicists, Vandana Shiva: "Democracy is not merely an electoral ritual but the power of people to shape their destiny, determine how their natural resources are owned and utilized, how their thirst is quenched, how their food is produced and distributed, and what health and education systems they have" (2002: xv). Shiva's advocacy for systemic accountability is a good reminder that the advent of greater democracy has the effect of placing limits on top-down, unaccountable power. Therefore, as progressive social work educators, social service providers, and activists, we are on the right track in resisting and challenging class privilege by pushing to expand the scope and effectiveness of our democratic institutions (Klein and Yalnizyan 2010; LaBerge 2010). Then too, as we

challenge the racialized and colonized privileges of class, we meet
other sources of systemic inequalities.

MALE PRIVILEGE

Mary O'Brien, a major contributor to feminist analysis, calls attention
to the fundamental importance of reproduction as a mode of production ignored by "malestream" thought because it has to do with
women as workers and producers, as key actors in production.
O'Brien points out that while class analysis is important, it is clearly
insufficient because it ignores the role of male supremacy: "Reproductive relations, on the other hand, never do manage to make history in
this interpretation. . . . This is pure patriarchal distortion; the act of
biological reproduction is *essentially* social and human, and forms of
the social relations of reproduction have as important an impact on
the social relations of production as vice versa" (1982: 254).

The devaluation of women's reproductive and other roles has
involved, among other things, a mix of restrictions: legal, economic,
social, and psychological. While different waves of feminism have
challenged these complex restrictions, many gender inequalities
remain. One of the most dangerous relics of patriarchal privilege is
the belief that men have the "right" to boss women around and to
punish them for "disobedience." A decade ago, about 350 shelters
existed across Canada where women and their children could seek
safety from abusive relationships. Today about 570 such social services are in place, and about 7,500 women and children live in them
on any given day. Meanwhile, hundreds of women and children are
being turned away on any given day because many shelters are filled
to capacity (Sauvé and Burns 2009: 5). Even when women have
their day in court, public attitudes are still prone to be one-sided. In
a study of the needs of social service users, Dawn Hemingway, Clarie
Johnson, and Brenda Roland write:

> With sexual violence, the level of scrutiny is such that the onus is
> entirely on the victim to prove her victimization and face the court of
> judgement about her character. Is she moral or immoral? Was she in
> the wrong place at the wrong time or did she "ask for it"? Myths

rooted in the oppression and exploitation of women declare that sexual assault is inevitable and part of the natural order of things; that women are assaulted only because they have poor judgement, put themselves in dangerous situations, follow a particular lifestyle, wear a short skirt, or have a drink or two. Even implementation of the 1983 Rape Shield Law . . . intended to restrict court testimony regarding a woman's sexual history or character, has failed to halt accusations and innuendo that blamed the victim. Women continue to be silenced. (2010: 84)

Painful experiences suffered by women are interconnected with other systemic inequalities such as racism, colonialism, and economic oppression. These oppressions are dynamically interconnected in ways that can deepen the sense of hopelessness and often mask their multiple sources. Though excluded from discussion in earlier times, issues identified by women of colour, lesbians, working-class women, and women with disabilities are now being heard in the women's movement and beyond it. Local and national feminist organizations, including women's shelters, have for some time been evolving a more diverse leadership (Barnoff 2001).

While diversity is now part of the women's movement, and while the women's movement has succeeded in pressing for the development of shelters and other support services, women are often excluded from major decision-making within large corporate and governmental institutions. The wage gap remains in place: "Women who work full-time year round earn only 71% of the average earnings of men working full time" (Townson 2009: 17; Canadian Feminist Alliance for International Action and Canadian Labour Congress 2010). In addition, feminists have pointed out that many women still suffer multiple jeopardy on a daily basis. As Martha Kuwee Kumsa defines it:

Women's multiple jeopardy refers to the double or triple day that most women assume when they take on paid work outside the home, unpaid care work in the home and unpaid, often unrecognized, advocacy, volunteer or activist work in the community. This compounded and often invisible workload can leave women feeling exhausted and exploited. (2007: 114)

Working within the women's movement, women developed innovative, fresh ways of helping women. Helen Levine, one of the early pillars in feminist social work in Canada, highlighted some features of feminist counselling:

> It has to do with an approach, a feminist way of defining women's struggles and facilitating change. It is no mysterious, professional technique. The focus is on women helping women in a non-hierarchical, reciprocal and supportive way. . . . It rests on a critical analysis of the sexism embedded in the theory and practice of the helping professions." (1982: 199)

The women's movement put feminist counselling into practice through the creation of shelters and counselling centres for abused women and their children, often on shoestring budgets. As time went on, the movement struggled to make services for women accessible and inclusive. Joan Laird, a U.S. social work educator, offers a definition of feminism: "Feminism represents an effort to understand how gender, race, class, ethnicity, and sexuality are constructed in social contexts of power, thereby dismantling hierarchies of privilege. Feminism is about locating the subjugated voice. It is about examining gendered voices and silences" (1995: 30).

Although the silencing of women's voices continues, the women's movement has opened up many arenas in which such silencing is being challenged. As a result many women have regained their voices, but there is still quite a way to go to achieve full gender equality. Along that road, feminists have helped us to recognize the intersections of gender with other oppressions (Feehan, Boettcher, and Quinn 2010: 64–68; Texler Segal and Martinez 2007). For example, using the lens of anti-racism, feminists have examined some of the root causes of the government's failure to implement a national child-care program. More specifically, Canadian immigration policies have been complicit by granting only temporary work visas when women of colour have been recruited from outside the country to come in and carry out domestic work. What this has done for some time now, according to feminist anti-racist scholar Enakshi Dua (1999: 246), is allow "the Canadian state to avoid the costs of a national childcare program" and enable middle-class women to participate in the labour force at the expense of the women of colour who get jobs as cheaply paid domestic workers.

GENDERED AGEISM

At times public policies demonstrate a certain success in improving people's well-being. In recent decades, the rate of poverty for Canadians over sixty-five years old has actually declined. But before we celebrate, the authors of the *Canadian Fact Book on Poverty* provide a caution: "Many elderly households have only been barely lifted above the poverty lines through a combination of federal elderly benefits. Thus, it should not be inferred from the improved poverty figures that the elderly are comfortably off. In fact, a large segment of the non-poor are nearly poor" (Ross, Scott, and Smith: 2000). In addition, the Special Senate Committee on Aging reported (2009: 93) that while the incomes of older people have generally increased over the past few decades, this trend has not resulted in the elimination of poverty among Canadian older people.

Furthermore, the intersections between gender inequality and ageism have persisted, and elderly women are still more than twice as susceptible to poverty as their male counterparts (Canada Without Poverty 2009: 4). Robert Butler, who is reputed to have coined the term "ageism," wrote that the younger generations "subtly cease to identify with their elders as human beings" (Canadian Network for the Prevention of Elder Abuse 2009: 1). The *Encyclopedia of Aging* presents Butler's definition of ageism "as a process of systematic stereotyping and discrimination against people because they are old." But ageism can apply to attitudes towards the young as well as the old. In any case, as the *Encyclopedia* puts it, "Ageism is manifested in a wide range of phenomena (on both individual and institutional levels), stereotypes and myths, outright disdain and dislike, or simply subtle avoidance of contact; discriminatory practices in housing, employment, and services of all kinds; epithets, cartoons and jokes" (Butler 2001: 38). According to the Canadian Network for the Prevention of Elder Abuse (2009: 4), this form of ageism makes it easier to de-humanize older adults, a practice that is pervasive in Canada.

Another consequence of ageism has been inadequate government support for social services in the area of long-term care. Sheila Neysmith, a feminist scholar at the University of Toronto, notes that budget cuts to health and social services have resulted in caring responsibilities for older adults being off-loaded onto families. She warns: "There is no evidence that family members can provide the type of care delivered by a qualified nursing assistant or home care worker. This off-loading onto families means that services are moved off the public stage and rendered invisible by relocating these in the private sphere of family responsibility." Much of the responsibility for caring work within families is still taken up by women because, as Neysmith notes, "Aging is a gendered process, so that women experience old age differently than men. One of these differences is that old women inhabit an aging body in a culture that devalues both" (2006: 401–2). In opposition to conventional economics, which fails to recognize the financial contribution of women in raising children, organizing their households, and caring for its adult members, Neysmith recommends that we un-gender caring labour and establish a universal caregiver model.

> Under such a model, employment policies and job descriptions would have caring related rights and benefits that complement the health and pension benefits today. Promotion ladders that do not allow for caring responsibilities could be challenged as discriminatory. Doing so is pivotal if women's citizenship claims are to be realized. This will happen only if caring for others is seen as central to the lives of all citizens, as central as holding down a paid job, participating in community affairs, paying taxes, and being a consumer. (408)

Such proposals for innovative policy changes are crucial if we are to undo oppression based on gender, age, and other forms of discrimination. The next step is to mobilize support for such changes. This also applies to a second definition of ageism: as a condition that creates an illegitimate sense of adult superiority by denying the humanity of young people, relegating them to the status of objects and making them targets for manipulation by adults. A young girl in a self-help group hesitatingly described her experience:

"The incest usually happened when my dad came home from the

bar. He'd be drunk and he'd come into the room and like we'd be in bed most of the time when he came home, because we knew he'd be drunk. So we'd go to bed and he'd come into the room and he'd sit on my bed and he'd put his hands on my breasts and my privates and I'd just – I'd wake up and I'd be really scared. And upset about it. And I'd wonder, well, what's going to happen? I don't want this to happen – and then he'd climb under the covers and start committing the incest and I'd tell him to stop – that it hurt – leave me alone – that I didn't like it – but he just wouldn't go away."

In this case a form of ageism collides with male privilege, and social service providers are expected to pick up the pieces.

HETEROSEXIST PRIVILEGE

Alongside colonial and racialized privileges – with the interwoven illegitimate benefits that are due to race, class, gender, and age – is sexual orientation, which is yet another major source of oppression and privilege. Marion Brown, Brenda Richard, and Leighann Wichman suggest a starting point for addressing lesbian, gay, transgender, two-spirit, intersex, and queer issues:

> Analysis of heterosexism and homophobia is where any discussion of the lives and challenges of queer people must begin, because the challenges faced and coping strategies utilized by queer people do not result from individual pathology, deficiency, or weakness, but rather result from the historic and contemporary discrimination, prejudice, and violence levelled against queer people and communities through the exploitative social constructs of heterosexism and homophobia. (2010: 157)

The McGill University Equity Subcommittee on Queer People (2010) provides definitions of heterosexism and homophobia:

> *Heterosexism* is based on societal values and personal belief systems which dictate that everyone is, or should be, heterosexual. Intentionally or unintentionally, our society privileges heterosexuality and heterosexual persons, and devalues, mistreats or discriminates against lesbian, gay, bisexual, two-spirited, queer and/or transgender persons and those perceived to be so.

Homophobia involves harassing, prejudicial treatment of, or negative attitudes about lesbian, gay, bisexual, queer, trans-identified, transgendered, inter-sexed or two-spirited (LGBQTT) persons and those perceived to be of these sexual orientations or gender identities. Homophobia includes a range of feelings and behaviours from discomfort and fear to disgust, hatred and violence.

Harassment and violence, in addition to exclusion due to heterosexist domination, has resulted in negative self-image and despair – so much so that gay and lesbian youth have a high risk of suicide (Centre for Suicide Prevention 2003). In addition, more than one-third of gay men and lesbians have experienced the physical violence of queer-bashing (O'Neill 2006: 338).

McGill University professor Shari Brotman and a team of researchers gave voice to the caregivers of gay and lesbian older adults who were receiving services from health and social service institutions in Montreal, Halifax, and Vancouver. The heterosexist discrimination experienced by these caregivers made it "increasingly difficult for caregiving partners to show affection, provide care when others were present, or gain recognition as the care receiver's spouse." As a result the care receivers became alienated from the services offered, and in an effort to protect or avoid discrimination themselves the caregivers may also refrain from making the most of the services available. The problem is that "the less care receivers make use of health and social services, the more is demanded of their caregivers" (Brotman et al. 2007: 498, 500).

The Equity Office of the University of British Columbia (2010) defines *transgendered, trans, or transidentified* as:

A person who identifies with a gender identity other than the one that was ascribed to their biological sex at birth; or a person who views their gender as more fluid than the strictly male or female gender categories allow. Also used as an umbrella term for transsexual, transgendered, cross-dressing, intersex, bi-gendered, genderqueer, multi-gendered, and androgynous people and those who don't identify with any gender labels. Trans persons may be gay, lesbian, bisexual, queer, two-spirit or heterosexual.

The term *two-spirit* or *two-spirited* people, as Fiona Meyer-Cook and

Diane Labelle point out (2004: 31), refers to Indigenous "gender identity and role, and includes gays, lesbians and other gender and sexuality identification." Coined in Winnipeg in 1990 at a Native American/First Nations gay and lesbian conference, "the term was adopted to reawaken the spiritual nature of the role these people are meant to play in their communities."

A bisexual person, according to one definition, is "a person who is romantically/sexually attracted to or involved with both men and women" (McGill University Equity Subcommittee on Queer People 2010).

While many social agencies have adopted policies that prohibit discrimination based on sexual orientation, for the most part social services do not provide services that support the lives of queer people. According to Brian O'Neill (2006: 341), "the pervasiveness of heterosexism" in social agencies has the effect of silencing the "discussion of sexual orientation, impeding the development of accessible and responsible programs, and leaving decisions regarding service delivery to individual workers." All of that in turn means that clients may not receive the appropriate service – and workers may well be left without guidance and support in their day-to-day jobs.

With the growing popularity of gay pride parades in certain parts of the country, with gay marriages being approved in a growing number of North American jurisdictions, and with an increasing recognition that hate laws need to be strengthened to protect queer people, heterosexist privileges are being increasingly challenged. Social work educator Samantha Wehbi's collection *Community Organizing against Homophobia and Heterosexism: The World through Rainbow-Colored Glasses* (2004) documents the worldwide nature of these challenges.

Some Canadian social agencies have set in place programs that specifically respond to the service delivery needs of queer people (Todd 2006: 292). Typically these social services have emerged within visible gay and lesbian communities, often located in urban environments, and as public attitudes have shifted towards a more progressive direction, such services have gained in credibility. The shifts in public opinion did not just happen on their own. They are the result of much hard work and dedication by members of sexually diverse community organizations, supported by allies in feminist and numerous other progressive social movements.

ABLEISM AND PRIVILEGE

About 12 per cent of Canadians are disabled in one way or another, and that condition has led to another social movement pushing for much-needed change. Professor Roy Hanes, a disability rights advocate at Carleton University, outlines a range of possible disabilities, including sensory impairments, such as blindness or deafness, psychiatric disabilities, developmental disabilities, learning disabilities, neurological disabilities, and mobility impairments. As Hanes indicates: "People can also become disabled as a result of many different factors, such as disease and/or injury. And, of course, many persons with disabilities have more than one impairment and therefore have more complex needs" (2006: 297).

Hanes and others have identified two competing disability theories that inform social work practice (Hanes 2006; Schwartz and O'Brien 2010). According to Hanes, the first theory views disability as primarily a medical problem that requires professional and medical assistance focused on rehabilitating the disabled individual. This rehabilitative/medical model also includes helping disabled individuals and those around them to pass through various stages of adjustment, such as denial, grief, and acceptance. This focus on the rehabilitative/medical model is the one most used by social services.

The second disability theory is the social oppression theory. Central to this approach is the recognition that "problems faced by people with disabilities are not the result of physical impairments alone, but are the result of the social and political inequality that exists between people with disabilities on the one hand and people without disabilities on the other."

In this view, it is society's failure to accommodate their needs that disables people. As a result, appropriate action focuses on the various barriers – economic, political, and social – that society has constructed that prevent equitable access to well-being (Barnes, Oliver, and Barton 2002: 5). These barriers persist in large part because of *ableism*, which denotes the consequences of "the belief in the superiority of people without disabilities over people with disabilities" (Hanes 2006: 310).

This belief in superiority produces privilege, such as the ability to construct a dominant set of attitudes and practices that over many years have stigmatized people with disabilities. Social work educator Judy MacDonald and hospital social worker Gaila Friars write about how people with disabilities have been treated historically: "They have been hidden away in family attics, institutionalized in state-based and private asylums, physically, emotionally, and sexually abused, sterilized against their will, socially segregated, and politically silenced" (2010: 138).

Again, much of the progress in breaking down the barriers facing people with disabilities is not due primarily to academic research, or to the work of social services, but rather to the political activism of people with disabilities (Barnes, Oliver, and Barton 2002: 4). Disabilities rights movements in various countries have contributed to a new, and crucial, sense of identity for people with disabilities: "Discovering our identity as disabled people is very, very important," state Ayesha Vernon and John Swain (2002: 85). "I think that it is probably the biggest success that the movement has been able to point to. It is our movement, nobody else owns it. We know who we are."

Part of this self-definition is the use of language. People who want to become allies to those who are marginalized for a variety of systemic reasons need to be open to the words and phrases recommended by the people most directly affected. More specifically, Mac-Donald and Friars point out that to be respectful, we need to further shift our language "by deconstructing terms such as mentally retarded, crippled, or mad and replacing them with people-first language. 'People with disabilities' puts the person first while identifying disability as one characteristic, while 'disabled persons' highlights the disability issues" (2010: 140).

MacDonald and Friars (2010: 140) advocate writing the word "disability" as: "(dis)Ability: '(dis)' to respect the person's social and physical connection with disability, and 'Ability' to highlight the creative and innovative ways of dealing with societal barriers."

There is also a growing recognition of how ableism intersects with other areas of privileges or oppressions, and of how these different facets need to connect (Sterling-Collins 2009). Research into the views of lesbians and bisexual women with (dis)Abilities, for instance, has indicated that many of them see themselves as being marginalized by lesbian and gay groups; according to Vernon and Swain (2002: 82), they "have experienced alienation rather than nurturing and support from the lesbian and gay community." People with (dis)Abilities and Black and ethnic minority people experience high unemployment rates and concentration in low-paid and low-skilled jobs. To gain awareness of the complexities facing people with (dis)Abilities, progressive social service providers need to take into account the intersecting barriers that include heterosexism, ableism, and racism.

SOCIAL JUSTICE AND SOCIAL SERVICES

The privileges and various systemic inequalities that are generated by society's structures and narratives have an impact on all of us. At the same time, we as individuals are not merely passive recipients of these political and personal dynamics. On the contrary, as individuals, we have our own capacity to respond – that is, to accept – or to resist, or question, what we are presented with.

Working for social justice is a continuing, unending process, not just an immediate goal or a once and for all event. Social justice calls for the dismantling of all oppressions and undue privileges. But social justice is about more than just dismantling injustice. It is also about constructing equitable personal/political/economic/social realities based on values such as caring, authentic democracy, and fairness. This process is sometimes called *social transformation*.

Social services are institutions that are officially supposed to improve people's lives. We help older adults write claims for necessary financial supplements. We help children find their way through difficult family situations. We provide shelter for women fleeing abusive relationships. We help palliative care patients who are facing death. We may also help a service user become an outspoken leader in one of the social movements committed to equity.

But these positives are only part of the picture. Much like other institutions in Canadian society, social services reproduce and perpetuate a variety of systemic privileges and oppressions, ranging from racism to ableism. Most social services are bureaucracies organized along hierarchical lines. They have rules to follow and funding conditions that prescribe the services to be provided. Whether funded by governments or charities, social services are usually answerable to affluent elites who often view their own privileges as entitlements.

At the same time, social services are contested terrain, meaning that a number of service providers, service users, and their allies are fighting back (Baines 2007a; Ferguson 2008; Hick et al. 2010; Kinewesquao and Wade 2009; Lavallée and Poole 2009; LaRose 2009; Mullaly 2010; Sinclair, Hart, and Bruyere 2009; Social Work Action Network 2010; Strega and Carriere 2009). In resisting the consequences of multiple oppressions, many social work educators and social service practitioners are attempting to address the root causes of exploitation and oppression in our society.

Feminist social work educator Lisa Barnoff writes about the need to include ourselves in this process, not in the sense of taking over the issues, but in recognizing that injustices are not just "out there" (2002: 328). Donna Baines states: "While addressing where one is placed on a multi-level continuum of privilege and oppression, it is equally important to understand, critique and improve how one *uses* that privilege to challenge oppression in everyday life" (2007b: 25). These new and better forms of social work are emerging alongside other practical initiatives within social services, and alongside grass-roots networks and diverse social movements – such as the efforts by Indigenous organizations and their allies to press for justice for First Nations, Métis, and Inuit peoples in Canada. Progressive community-based voices are calling for a restructuring of oppressive institutions both locally and globally. Our need for such a transformation – as well as different progressive responses to this need – is further documented in the following pages.

3 ROOTS: EARLY ATTITUDES

Mary Dowding 514 King St. E. and husband. No children. says can't get work. fancy they don't want it. no reason why they should be in want. Recommend a little starvation until self-help engendered, probably drink.

— from notes of a volunteer visitor, Toronto 1882

When I was still a student in social work, the history of the welfare state was presented as a process of evolution whereby society gradually recognized its responsibility to the "less fortunate" or "underprivileged." In fact, nowhere in my high school or university education was there any mention of how today's institutions in North America were built upon the ashes of two colossal human catastrophes.

In 1492, when the European conquest of the "New World" began, a population of about 100 million Indigenous people lived in the vast terrain of what is now North, Central, and South America. The violent invasion and subsequent European settlement, including extensive massacres of Indigenous peoples, led to the introduction of wave upon wave of disease – smallpox, yellow fever, cholera, and others – to which the Indigenous peoples had previously had no exposure and therefore had built up little or no immunity. These diseases inflicted a devastating toll. By 1600 an estimated ninety million of the original inhabitants of the Americas had died. Writer Ronald Wright states, "It was the greatest mortality in history. To conquered and conqueror alike, it seemed as though God really was on the white man's side" (2000: 13–14).

The second event, also fuelled by greed, the drive for profits, and racism, was the violent wrenching of African people away from their homes to become slaves in the New World. Historian Donald Spivey argues:

> Europe systematically raped the African continent. Whether one accepts the often cited figure of twelve million Africans killed, taken, or otherwise lost to the slave trade, or the more likely figure of forty million and more killed, taken, or otherwise lost to the slave trade, the impact was catastrophic for Africa and monumental for European coffers and the New World. (2003: 59)

These two catastrophes have a strong connection with each other, and they are also linked with a third historical phenomenon: the cruel and abusive treatment of poverty-stricken and other "inferior" Europeans at the hands of their own rulers. English law in 1531, certainly, was blunt about what would happen to the less fortunate. A person considered to be one of society's "ill-begotten" group of "idle poor, ruffelers, sturdy vagabonds and valiant beggars" was "to be tied to the end of a cart naked and to be beaten with whips throughout the same market-town or other place til his body be bloody by reason of such whipping." As if this was not enough, this unfortunate would "also have the upper part of the grissle of his right ear clean cut off" (de Schweinitz 1943: 21–22).

At the same time as brutality was inflicted on jobless men, women were violently persecuted under suspicion of witchcraft. The accusation was focused mainly on spinsters and widows (that is, those women without male "protection") who might try to achieve a degree of personal independence. In doing this they posed a threat to the monopoly of male authority in intellectual, moral, economic, and religious spheres. Mary Daly documents (1978: 180) the belief current in 1486 that "All witchcraft comes from carnal lust which is in women insatiable." This belief, combined with the self-righteous suspicion that some women were in league with the devil, served to justify witch hunts and the subsequent cruelty, torture, and killings of large numbers of women (Daly 1978: 178–222). In Spain at about the same time the Inquisition was in full swing, indicating that European leaders did not restrict their cruelty to women or to the poor. Anyone suspected of ever so slight deviations from official Catholic teachings could be subjected to investigation, with lethal consequences. Furthermore, if you were part of the Jewish community, you could be a target for forcible conversion or be deported or face death (Paris 1995). The contempt and hatred for Jews have a long history in Christian Europe – a history that became a rehearsal for the genocidal policies carried out when the Nazis rose to power in Germany during the twentieth century.

Periodically rebellions occurred in which the targets of violence were reversed and aimed at the privileged – as in the French Revolution or even earlier. In sixteenth-century France, for example, the general population suffered through a time of bad harvests, extreme hunger, and famine that caused countless people to leave their farms. Many of them migrated to the growing city of Lyons, where they begged or found casual work at low wages. With the poor harvests the townsfolk found the price of grain doubling or quadrupling in a matter of days, and they couldn't afford to buy bread. Then, as Canadian anti-poverty activist Jean Swanson notes: "In 1529 the starving people of Lyons took over the city, forcing the wealthy to flee to a monastery for their own protection. They looted the homes of the rich and sold the grain from a public and a church granary" (2001: 30). In an attempt to avoid such rebellions, the elite developed a crude welfare system, taxing the well-off in Lyons to supplement church contributions for the poor; every Sunday food and money were distributed to the needy.

In time some European laws softened. In England, instead of being beaten and mutilated, the unemployed (or the "able-bodied," as they were called) were imprisoned and forced to work in jail-like institutions called houses of correction, "There to be straightly kept, as well in diet as in work, and also punished from time to time" (de Schweinitz 1943: 26). Influenced by the church, the state was somewhat less harsh to the "impotent poor," that is, the deserted mothers with children, the "lame," the "demented," the old, and the sick. These unfortunates could in seventeenth-century England receive limited assistance from officials who were called the "overseers" of the poor and who had been appointed to their positions by justices of the peace or magistrates. Two centuries later this division between worthy and unworthy poor remained, with both groups often ending up in workhouses or poorhouses, which had replaced the houses of correction. Social critic Charles Dickens attacked these workhouses in his novel *Oliver Twist*.

American feminist Mimi Abramovitz examined the impact of U.S. social welfare policy on the lives of women from colonial times to the late twentieth century. Her book *Regulating the Lives of Women* notes that a patriarchal standard about what women should or should not do "has been used to distinguish among women as deserving or undeserving of aid since colonial times" (1988: 40).

In Canada, governments imported the traditions of France and England. While Quebec's government left it to the Catholic Church to provide assistance and education to the poor, the colonial administration in the Maritimes saw to the construction of a workhouse in 1759, where "for many years whipping, shackling, starvation, and other necessary inducements were used to correct the behaviour of the idle, vagrant, or incorrigible inmates" (Bellamy 1965). Public auctions of paupers also took place. In 1816 in the Upper Canada village of Delaware, an indigent widow was auctioned off to the lowest bidder. What happened was that paupers were "boarded out" in a sort of foster-home system. The auction was to see who would charge the municipality *least* for their keep; the successful bidder would expect to more than make up his cost by the work he would get out of the pauper.

Social historian Allan Irving documented the introduction of welfare to Upper Canada in the 1830s by Sir Francis Bond Head, the lieutenant-governor, who believed that "workhouses should be made repulsive . . . if any would not work for relief, neither he should eat" (1989: 17). Although workhouses were not developed everywhere in English Canada, the local jails served the same purpose: "Jails became a type of poorhouse – a catch-all for a variety of social problems" that included people of all ages who were in poverty, homeless, or had a mental illnesses, or were found guilty of minor or major crimes (Guest 1980: 12).

This history of Canada's responses to people who were barely surviving due to poverty or other oppressive conditions evolved on the heels of the horrific dispossession of the Indigenous peoples. Colonial violence, racism, and exploitation not only shattered the economic self-sufficiency of the First Nations peoples, but also created havoc with their communal and family life (Albert 1991). The colonial takeover of land in North America and the attitude of contempt towards the First Nations were echoed in sixteenth- and seventeenth-century England by the enclosures of common land used by peasant farmers. Writer and filmmaker Richard Bocking outlines the seizure of land in England:

> "The commons" was the name used in medieval England to describe parcels of land that were used "in common" by peasant farmers, very few of whom owned enough land to survive on. Their lives depended on access to and use of shared land that provided many necessities: pasture for their oxen or livestock, water in streams, ponds or wells, wood and fuel from a forest.
>
> The land was probably owned by a titled notable, but the importance of the commons to the survival of the population was so obvious that strict rules, recognized by the courts, required landowners to ensure that the commons was available for use by peasant farmers. . . .
>
> Landowners began to think of how much richer they could be if they could remove the "commoners" and use the land themselves. They began to plant hedges or otherwise bar the way onto lands that had been used and depended upon by nearby families for centuries. This practice became known as "enclosure." Eventually the British Parliament bowed to the will of wealthy landowners and passed Enclosure Acts that stripped commoners of their property rights. (2003: 26)

As English farmers were shoved off the commons, they moved into big cities, looking for work. By the nineteenth century, England had brutal factory conditions, including long hours of child labour. Trade unions were illegal, women had no vote, and the living conditions of the working class were abysmal. The owners of industry and commerce believed that it was their superior moral character, not their economic structures, that was responsible for the large gap between rich and poor, men and women, Whites and non-Whites. Such was their smugness that some of the well-to-do genuinely felt that the pauper class needed only proper moral instruction to be raised out of their woeful condition.

If poor men had few rights during this era, women were seen as chattels, or as the property of men, with no separate existence of their own.

Just as the position of people living in poverty was a subordinate one, the same was true of people of colour. During an age when many people still supported slavery, there were ample theories to justify assumptions about the "superiority" of a highly privileged upper class and indeed of the growing middle class, and the "natural rights" of the men in these classes to subordinate others.

One form of justification was the growing emphasis on "scientific thinking," which by the nineteenth century was used to explain why people occupied different ranks and status. Theories such as the survival of the fittest, with arguments about the extinction of certain animal species and the continuation of other species, were applied to thinking about people and economic status. Aristocratic men of privilege, as a consequence, were viewed as the "fittest," possessing the most desirable of human traits. This group of "superior" beings included men rather than women, Whites rather than non-Whites, the able-bodied rather than people with (dis)Abilities, property owners rather than servants. The evidence for the aristocracy's "moral superiority," presumably, consisted of their extraordinary privileges and their ability to have their commands carried out (Macarov 1978).

Conversely, it followed that the poor and the powerless possessed the least desirable traits. Those who were paupers, due to either illness or (dis)Ability, or to old age, gender prejudices, low-paying jobs, or unemployment, became viewed as "inferior" – a designation still very much with us to this day.

The brutalities of the workhouses in England brought agitation for change by the working class and reformers in England. But a Royal Commission established in 1834 to study the conditions of the poor strongly recommended the continuation of workhouses for the poor, including the continuation of harsh conditions. The reason these privileged commissioners gave: "Every penny bestowed, that tends to render the condition of the pauper more eligible than that of the independent laborer, is a bounty on indolence and vice" (Marcus 1978: 51).

The Royal Commission believed that it had discovered a way of both aiding the needy and protecting the system. It would accomplish this by extending benefits to the poor at a level that was clearly less than the wage of the poorest-paid employee. There was to be no room for questioning whether the lowest wage was a fair wage or a poverty wage – nor was there room to ask, how does the exploitation of the poor stem from unjust privilege? The net effect was to legitimate these lowest wages by focusing on the incentive of the working poor. In addition this approach also created the illusion of freedom. The poor were to be given "choices." Work at abysmal wages, or enter the workhouse, or die of starvation.

To implement that report, six hundred more workhouses were built throughout England between 1834 and 1850 (Corrigan and Corrigan 1980: 14). It was the kind of thinking, fashioned by rich, White men of privilege, that still reverberates today within social assistance offices across Canada.

SOCIAL WORK: THE BEGINNINGS

In the late nineteenth century, when social work began as an embryonic profession in London, the main movers of charity accepted the established division between worthy and unworthy poor. There was a certain sympathy for the worthy poor, but for the unworthy – the able-bodied poor or the unemployed – it was still felt that the full rigour of the workhouse should be applied. Welfare state expansion tended to focus on these unworthy poor, often women: "unwed" mothers, "promiscuous ladies," "irresponsible" wives, and so on. This left the worthy to be aided by the more traditional charitable organizations, outside the purview of the state.

The idea of more systematic social assistance took on an added sense of urgency when members of the affluent class noticed that socialism was becoming more appealing to the factory workers. Furthermore, the rich donors resented being pestered for donations to the many separate charities. Along with this resentment, there was the suspicion that many paupers were lying about their circumstances in an effort to collect greater amounts of relief from more than one charity.

As a result, a new organization was formed in 1869 in London: the Society for Organizing Charitable Relief and Repressing Mendicancy. It was soon renamed the Charity Organization Society (C.O.S.). It offered to co-ordinate the various charities and advocated a thorough investigation of each application for charity. Such co-ordination and investigation came to symbolize "scientific charity," which borrowed ideas from the emerging social sciences and from factory management. With these innovations, charity leaders held out the promise of imposing efficiency upon the charity process. Through investigation of applicants, fraudulent claims would be weeded out. And for the truly needy, the cause of their poverty would be discovered (Lappin 1965).

The C.O.S. approach became popular and spread to other locations. At the operational level, the C.O.S. provided "friendly visitors" from the upper class who volunteered to visit poor families. So much importance was placed on developing a co-operative, helpful relationship between the help-giver and the help-receiver that it was the relationship itself that came to be viewed as the best form of assistance to the poor. Since the C.O.S. leaders believed that financial aid would be wasted on the poor, their motto became "Not alms, but a friend."

In the late nineteenth century the C.O.S. was transplanted to North America (Popple 1983: 75). The following advice was given to friendly visitors on how to develop co-operative, helpful relationships with the poor: "You go in the full strength and joy and fire of life; full of cheer and courage; with a far wider knowledge of affairs; and it would be indeed a wonder if you could not often see why the needy family does not succeed, and how to help them up" (Lubove 1965: 13). Given the assumption that the poor were morally inferior, it was logical that assistance became defined as moral advice on how to uplift the poor into becoming better individuals. It was conceded that as time went on, morally uplifted individuals might even escape their poverty.

Social workers, however, did not directly replace the well-to-do volunteer. There was an intermediate step, stemming from the nature of the C.O.S. Again, at the operational level, the C.O.S. format consisted not only of wealthy volunteers, but also of paid employees called "agents" who were often from the working class (Lappin 1965: 64). These "agents" were poorly paid and low-status technicians. Initially they were few in number, but as the quantity of cases grew and far exceeded the number of volunteers, more agents were hired and they all carried larger parts of the workload. This group of employees became the forerunner of the modern social worker.

While a humanitarian impulse was present, the early days of social work were infused by negative attitudes towards the less fortunate. Most thinkers on social questions at the time believed that the proper role of the state was to be minimal – to maintain public institutions for criminals, the "insane," and the "absolutely unfit." Those who were simply poor or unemployed or "handicapped" in some way were to be left to the charitable institutions or, more likely, to their own devices. The prevailing attitude was that most people who were living in poverty and who, for instance, resorted to begging were out-and-out frauds, and that it was harmful to aid these people (Copp 1974: 115).

Still, some of the early social workers had a more compassionate view. They refused to accept as "given" the idea that the oppressive living conditions of new immigrants in the urban centres of North America could not be changed. For example, Jane Addams, who founded Chicago's Hull house in 1889, became legendary for her advocacy for public health and decent housing. She inspired others, both inside and outside of social work, to begin recognizing that the social environment external to an individual was also a cause of poverty. Yet this recognition of oppression was limited. During this period of history, as scholar and activist Akua Benjamin notes: "First Nations peoples faced genocide. Queers were forced into the closet. During Jane Addam's era and beyond, Blacks were being lynched with the tolerance or participation of the law. Thus, while radical forms of social work resisted oppression in some communities, oppression found expression in the everyday life of many other communities" (2007: 199).

Social work researcher Carol Baines documents how caring for others was seen as women's "natural work." In a world of patriarchal privilege, this female caring was undervalued. Baines also describes how a move towards social work professionalism at the turn of the twentieth century meant more reliance on male supervisors and more specialization, and less emphasis on support networks with other women (1998: 59–60). These early social agencies found themselves answerable to wealthy male philanthropists or politicians. The result, according to Jennifer Dale and Peggy Foster (1986: 38), was that "the new professions were made up of middle-class women who were very much involved in the social control of working class mothers." During those years First Nations people received little or nothing of these "benefits," while their travels in and out of Indian reservations were tightly controlled by the Canadian government's Indian agents.

The relative invisibility of other systemic barriers, such as those posed by class privilege, racism, ableism, and heterosexism, reinforced conservative ideologies among Canada's early social workers. The model adopted in social work, as social historian Terry Copp puts it, was "stern charity, charity designed to be as uncomfortable and demeaning as possible." Copp analyses the case of Montreal, which in 1901 was home to a great variety of charitable institutions organized along ethnic and religious lines: "fifteen houses of refuge, thirteen outdoor relief agencies, fourteen old age homes, eleven orphanages, eighteen 'moral and educational institutions,' and more than a score of other miscellaneous charitable agencies" (1974: 106).

Along the same lines, when the Depression created massive unemployment in the 1930s, social work leaders were suspicious of granting relief payments to the poor. One leader, Charlotte Whitton, argued that instead of paying money to needy parents, the state should remove children from their homes. She believed that many of the mothers were unfit as parents, and so: "The dictates of child protection and sound social work would require cancellation of allowance, and provision for the care of the children under guardianship and authority" (Guest 1980: 57).

There was also fear. At a January 1932 meeting one of the local

branches of the Canadian Association of Social Workers reported
(1932: 117, 119): "Social workers are paid by the capitalist group,
for the most part, in order to assist the under-privileged group. Thus
organized support of political issues would be very difficult if not
dangerous . . . because of the danger of attempting too radical
changes, since we are paid by the group who would resent such
changes most."

In Canada the expansion of the welfare state occurred due to
several converging factors. The dislocation during and after the First
World War – with the need for support both of injured soldiers and
of families left behind – brought some initial forays into expanding
state intervention. A greater force was increasing labour turmoil and
worker dissatisfaction with brutally unfair conditions, as the urban
population grew and industrialization continued. In the first three
decades of the century, as Copp writes:

> All of the accepted norms of society were being called into question by
> the growing complexity and disorder of the industrial system. Mon-
> treal was being transformed into a sprawling ugly anthill. Frequent
> strikes and the growth of labour unions seemed to foreshadow class
> warfare on a European scale. . . . The fundamental social problem was
> poverty, massive poverty, created by low wages and unemployment.
> For individuals, direct assistance limited hunger and prevented starva-
> tion, but the small section of the working class which regularly came
> into contact with organized charity was too often confronted with the
> "alms of friendly advice" and too seldom helped to achieve security.
> (1974: 127)

In 1919 Winnipeg experienced a general strike when thirty thousand
workers left their jobs to fight for the principle of collective bargaining, better wages, and the improvement of working conditions. In
this case the state proved only too eager to intervene, refusing to talk
with unions but sending in Mounted Police and federal troops. The
state clearly came down on the side of the privileged – manufacturers, bankers, businessmen – and revealed a distinct distaste for ideas
and actions involving workers' rights.

Police forces were also used against the institutions of Indigenous people – who were still portrayed by the insulting depictions of

"savages," "lacking in culture" and "possessing no worthy structures of their own in the first place." A House of Commons (1983) Special Committee on Indian Self-Government sadly documented what colonialism had destroyed.

> The Iroquois (as they were known by the French) or Six Nations (as the English called them) or the Haudenosaunee (*People of the Longhouse*, as they called themselves) have a formalized constitution, which is recited every five years by elders who have committed it to memory. It provides for a democratic system in which each extended family selects a senior female leader and a senior male leader to speak on its behalf in their respective councils. Debates on matters of common concern are held according to strict rules that allow consensus to be reached in an efficient manner, thus ensuring that the community remains unified. A code of laws, generally expressed in positive admonitions rather than negative prohibitions, governs both official and civil behaviour. . . .
>
> The Canadian government suppressed the Haudenosaunee government by jailing its leaders and refusing to give it official recognition. In 1924, the council hall at the Six Nations Reserve was raided by the Royal Canadian Mounted Police (RCMP). All official records and symbols of government were seized.

This assault against Indigenous people was in line with the assimilationist policies of Canadian political and business leaders. With the Depression of the 1930s, working-class militancy spawned a series of protests, including the famous On-to-Ottawa Trek, when four thousand angry workers marched across Canada to present their grievances to Parliament. During this time in the United States, social workers known as the Rank and File Movement joined militant labour activists who, similar to left-wing political groups in Canada, were openly calling for an end to capitalism (Heinonen and Spearman 2001: 16–18).

As a result of the opposition, leading industrialists began to grant concessions to the labour movement's advocacy for old age pensions and unemployment insurance. Reluctantly they supported some expansion of the state into social welfare, provided it was understood that capitalism itself would not be threatened. Sir

Charles Gordon, president of the Bank of Montreal, wrote to Prime Minister R.B. Bennett in 1934 to support the idea of unemployment insurance: "May I suggest to you that for our general self-preservation some such arrangement will have to be worked out in Canada and that if it can be done soon so much the better" (Finkel 1977: 349). Not everyone in power agreed, but enough of them were persuaded to endorse an expansion of social welfare. When the federal government decided it was time to adopt unemployment insurance and other social programs, the same prime minister reminded business leaders why an expansion of the welfare state was necessary: "A good deal of pruning is sometimes necessary to save a tree and it would be well for us to remember there is considerable pruning to be done if we are to save the fabric of the capitalist system" (Findlay 1982: 9).

To further camouflage this "pruning" of the capitalist system, business and government officials began to argue that our civilization had developed a capacity for compassionate responses to the needy, that "humane values" constituted the foundation of Canadian society, and that social programs were the manifestations of the society's concern for helping one's "fellow man" (they were perhaps less certain about women).

Within this rationale, political support was consolidated for Canada's income security programs. The first old age pension was introduced in 1927. Its payment of $20 a month was subject, as social policy researcher Dennis Guest puts it, "to a strict and often humiliating means test – proof that poor-law attitudes still influenced Canadian political leaders in the 1920s" (1985: 1723).

In the following years workers' compensation for injuries, public assistance, child welfare, and public health programs were created or expanded (Struthers 1983; Irving 1981; Moscovitch 1986). The 1950s and 1960s saw a substantial growth in social programs, with the federal government playing a key role in the funding of new, universal, old age security payments, an expanded employment insurance program, an evolving medicare approach, and additional social services geared to low-income Canadians.

Outspoken social workers also criticized the ever-present opposition to social welfare. Bertha Capen Reynolds, a radical social worker in the United States, wrote in 1950:

> We have noted that the interests which oppose really constructive social work constitute only a small minority of the whole population, but influence a much larger sector through their ownership of newspaper chains and control of radio broadcasting. Many hard-working folk who sincerely want people in trouble to have a fair break are frightened by propaganda to the effect that the country is being ruined by taxes to support a "welfare state," and that people on relief are "chiselers" and social workers "sob sisters." (1951: 165)

Yet even the years of welfare-state expansion saw severe shortages of social services. Bridget Moran, a social worker based in Prince George, B.C., during the 1950s and 1960s, documented her experience. In 1963 she wrote to the premier of British Columbia:

> I could not face my clients for yet another year without raising my voice to protest for them the service they are going to get from me. I have no excuse except desperation for what follows. . . . Every day, here and across the province social workers are called upon to deal with seriously disturbed children. We have no psychiatrists, no specially-trained foster parents, no receiving or detention homes to aid us. We place children in homes that have never been properly investigated, we ignore serious neglect cases because we have no available homes. (1992: 69–70)

As social work was growing as a profession, child welfare agencies hired social workers to protect children who were abused or neglected – which led, among other things, to that sorry chapter in social work history known as the "Sixties Scoop" (see chapter 2).

Feelings of resentment against social workers by Indigenous people were echoed by many people in low-income neighbourhoods, where social workers were called child-snatchers. These dynamics prompted social critics to weigh in. For example, U.S. community organizer Saul Alinsky argued over sixty years ago that social workers "come to the people of the slums under the aegis of benevolence and goodness, not to organize the people, not to help them rebel and fight their way out of the muck – NO! They come to get these people 'adjusted'; adjusted so they will live in hell and like it too" (1946: 82). An extreme view, perhaps, but one shared by many critics who see the conservative and colonial values of the past – the values of the poor laws, for example – as being simply recycled, modernized, and institutionalized within Canadian social services. These critics argue that the development of beliefs about helping are expressions of the system rather than challenges to it, that social programs are shaped by capitalism, patriarchy, and colonialism and other power relations based on inequality.

Canadian history provides all too many examples of how such power relations have shaped "assistance" to the detriment of the people being "helped." For example, people with (dis)Abilities were hardly "helped" by the sterilization laws introduced by most Canadian provinces in the 1920s and 1930s. As part of the eugenics movement, which assumed that "better" breeding would create a "better" society, thousands of people with (dis)Abilities, often people with intellectual (dis)Abilities, were sterilized (MacDonald and Friars 2010:139).

In the 1950s women were hardly "helped" by the psychiatric treatment of families, a treatment that highlighted faulty mothering as the key cause of emotional disturbances. Helen Levine documented some of the oppressive assumptions made by psychiatrists at that time: "The message is that if mothers/wives were doing their motherwork of meeting the personal and sexual needs of men and fathers, incest would not occur" (1982: 196).

Gay men, lesbians, and bisexual and transgendered people were hardly "helped" by professionals who diagnosed them as being mentally ill due to their sexuality. Children were hardly "helped" in various Canadian orphanages and institutions where they had to endure all kinds of abuse. When these children were Indigenous, and/or female, or queer, and when some of them had (dis)Abilities, the intersecting vulnerabilities combined as targets for further harm.

But the social services provided by the state have been more than a method of social control. They also represent battles fought and won over the years by many people. Side by side with domination came resistance. Frances Fox Piven and Richard Cloward studied the mass protests and strikes by the labour, civil rights, and welfare rights movements in the United States during the twentieth century. They concluded that when there is wide public support for protest movements, the privileged may offer an expansion of social programs in a bid to restore stability (1979: 4). According to this analysis, the growth of the welfare state can be understood as stemming in part from a militant labour movement and a consequent fear of revolution, which together prompt concessions to a population that needs to be convinced that capitalism is capable of caring for its social casualties and of curbing its worst excesses. In this sense the welfare state plays the role of legitimizing a political and economic system under attack.

During the 1960s and 1970s the system was increasingly challenged not only for its racism and economic exploitation but also for its exclusions based on identities such as gender and sexuality. As a result of these challenges, further progress towards equity, though limited, was nevertheless achieved. Feminists and the women's movement broke occupational barriers and created women's shelters and feminist counselling centres that influenced social work education. In 1973, for example, the American Psychiatric Association removed homosexuality from its list of mental disorders. Sexual minorities created networks of social services and in 1982 section 15 of the Canadian Charter of Rights and Freedoms prohibited discrimination based on sexual orientation (Bielmeier 2002: 208). That same year people with physical and mental (dis)Abilities were also included in the Charter of Rights (Dunn 2003: 206). (Dis)Abilities rights organizations engaged in court battles; in 1997 the Supreme Court of Canada stated:

> Historical disadvantage has to a great extent been shaped and perpetuated by the notion that disability is an abnormality or flaw. As a result, disabled persons have not generally been afforded the "equal concern, respect and consideration" that s. 15(1) of the Charter demands. Instead, they have been subjected to paternalistic attitudes of pity and charity, and their entrance into the social mainstream has been conditional upon their emulation of able bodied norms. (*Eldridge v. British Columbia* 1997)

In 2010 Canada ratified the United Nations Convention on the Rights of Persons with Disabilities, calling on its signatories to change or abolish laws, policies, and practices that permit discrimination against individuals with (dis)Abilities. But while this ratification may seem like major progress, as newspaper columnist Carol Goar notes, "Canada has failed to live up to the standards of other UN conventions it has ratified: on climate change, the rights of the child, the elimination of discrimination against women and the protection of the rights of migrants workers" (2010: A15).

These limited victories won through the courts and other institutions came as a result of sustained educational and political campaigns by separate social movements that had minimal contact with each other. During the 1970s and 1980s the formations began to change. Instead of competing about which oppression was the most damaging, social activists came to recognize the value of analysis and action that drew on the interconnections between various oppressions.

By the 1980s many feminists were making these links more explicit. In their book *Feminist Organizing for Change*, Nancy Adamson, Linda Briskin, and Margaret McPhail (1988: 98–99) developed a synthesis of major forms of domination: "Neither class, gender, nor race is privileged as *the* primary source of oppression. Rather, the fundamental interconnections between the structures of political and economic power – in our society, capitalism – and the organization of male power – what we might refer to as 'patriarchal relations' – [are] emphasized." That is why these authors highlight the term *patriarchal capitalism*, to illuminate "the class nature of women's oppression, the impact of racism and heterosexism, and the role of the state in reinforcing women's oppression" (99).

Still, just when there seemed to be a new potential for the diverse networks, including social service providers, to consolidate their limited gains and work closer together to achieve greater equity, these hopes, with a few exceptions, were shattered by a countervailing force in North America and in much of the Western world. Having convinced the public to equate "waste and inefficiency" with government, corporate leaders used their influence to lead a reckless charge for tax cuts, deregulation, and speculative investments.

The result was the construction of an artificial financial bubble that burst in 2008, sending the world's economies into a tailspin. Social programs, which had already been squeezed due to tax cuts, became even more vulnerable as political leaders used public funds to prop up teetering business corporations. Despite these efforts, unemployment worsened along with an increase in precarious, part-time, and low-paying jobs, all of which contributed to greater poverty. The financial cuts to social programs by various levels of government put considerable pressure on social service providers to carry higher caseloads to deal with more service users trapped in more desperate situations. Some social agencies were shut down due to a lack of funds; others continued to barely limp along. Social work education, in a new century, has been presented yet again with new challenges. How will it respond?

Diverging Schools of Altruism

Social workers promote social fairness and the equitable distribution of resources, and act to reduce barriers and expand choice for all persons, with special regard for those who are marginalized, disadvantaged, vulnerable, and/or have exceptional needs.

— Canadian Association of Social Workers, Code of Ethics

A strong emphasis on altruism pervades social work. Most students who enter social work are eager to help others. In Canada over 23,000 students a year are enrolled in various community colleges and universities that offer social work and social service work programs (Canadian Association for Social Work Education 2009; Canadian Association of University Teachers 2007: 22). In addition, colleges and universities are offering diplomas and degrees in a whole series of social service specializations, such as disabilities studies, youth and child welfare work, gerontology, addictions counselling, correctional officer training, women's shelters, and community work. As a reason for choosing these programs of study students frequently say, "I want to help people." There is still that selfless quality of seeing other people's needs as a priority for action.

Why do some individuals become highly motivated to enter a profession that is so steeped in altruism? Typically, there are many reasons, some of which are unique to specific individuals, while other reasons are shared by many people. In my own case, as a child I was hidden in Belgium during the Nazi genocide of Jews. My parents did not survive. After World War II, when I was nine years old my mother's sister arranged for me to come and live with her and her family in Canada. My childhood years were characterized by abrupt dislocation and a repressed sense of loss. With the help of some caring family members, I somehow managed to heal suffi-ciently from my childhood trauma, and to develop a sense of bal-ance: so much so that in later years I was frequently able to offer emotional support to others. When I entered social work I felt I had found a haven of sanity in a world filled with conflict, injustices, and cynicism.

When I went to university, in the 1960s, most social work stu-dents were from the middle class and White. That situation has changed to some degree over the past fifty years. Today social work programs in community colleges and universities reflect greater cul-tural and class diversity. In Canada many students hold part-time jobs, and many take out loans to finance their university education: their average debt load on completion of their studies is over $37,000 (Canadian Association of University Teachers 2009: 38). At the same time the Canadian trend towards higher tuition fees threat-ens to narrow the student population to the more privileged socio-economic classes reminiscent of previous times.

Altruism is also common to other human service professions. Whether it is nursing patients back to health or teaching children to read and write or understand algebra, a deep sense of satisfaction often comes from one person helping another. Some researchers sug-gest that altruism has a biological basis and that mutual aid may be as much an instinct towards survival as the need to locate food (Okasha 2008).

What about social work help? What makes it unique? Social work education mixes in material from psychology and psychiatry, offering a gateway to the world of personal motives, subconscious drives, family dynamics, pathological responses, and on and on. It is exciting stuff. Students can and do apply these concepts to them-selves, their peers, and to others. But it does not end there. There is also the focus on the societal level. Materials and approaches from sociology, political science, and economics are selected, condensed, and applied to social welfare. Students learn about various income security schemes, law-making processes, and political pressures.

Again, it is heady stuff. And with Canadian governments spending billions of dollars per year on health and social programs, including pensions and other income security payments, students quickly get the feeling that they have arrived in the big leagues.

At the same time as social work continues to evolve as a profession, altruism has come under attack – so much so that social work educators, practitioners, and service users often feel as though they are swimming against a tide of hostile attitudes. On more than one occasion my own sense of altruism has been dismissed as being naïve, foolish, or just not in keeping with the tenor of the times. As I reflect about such dismissive attitudes, my observation is that altruism is being pushed to the sidelines by its very opposite – greed – which seems to have become a central pillar of the Western world.

Canadian writer Linda McQuaig refers to historian and anthropologist Karl Polanyi, who "made the provocative point that it is only in the last few centuries, and only in parts of the Western world, that greed and the endless pursuit of material gain have been given almost free rein." McQuaig's conclusion is that the centrality of greed has resulted in a massive negative transformation of society: "Polanyi went on to argue that this transformation was not some natural evolution, based on the reality of human nature, but rather was a deliberately imposed redesign of society, carried out by a small but powerful elite in order to enhance its own interests" (2001: 7).

Fortunately, this redesign was not total. On the contrary, the widespread media and commercial hype that encourages us to accept greed as a desirable value is being challenged in numerous ways. For example, rather than seeing greed as the primary engine for human behaviour, postmodernists tend to understand human nature as being influenced by a huge variety of motivations stemming from a multiplicity of differences in individual experiences, personalities, values, and narratives. For these and other reasons, social workers need not be apologetic as they act on altruistic values. In translating such values into practice, social workers employ different techniques, such as problem-solving, solution-seeking, and trauma-healing, to help people in crises and emergencies and to deal with everyday personal and social problems (Hick 2006: 19).

Yet as we act on our altruism, we can also stumble. Sometimes we make the mistake of assuming that if we honestly strive for the goal of human well-being, then service users will automatically be grateful. Reality suggests otherwise, as illustrated by a group of women living on social assistance who were asked to address students at the University of British Columbia. One of them recalled:

"When we told students in social work about our experiences, they were stunned. They figured it's a rainbow out there and all they have to do is say to clients, 'I'm on your side.' But it's not that easy. They were stunned to find that families on welfare were bitter, frustrated, and degraded. They didn't realize the strains, the hatred. Maybe they thought all clients liked social workers. They were surprised to hear about all those applications we're expected to fill out, all the lecturing we get about getting jobs. They didn't know that the jobs we could get pay so poorly they don't even cover the costs of day care and transportation. From my experience, social workers don't get down to the core – why children on welfare are feeling the way they are. Social workers are fast to blame the family, but they don't go to the roots of these frustrations. And a lot of it has to do with not having enough money."

CONFICTS INSIDE THE SOCIAL WORK CURRICULUM

Just as the push and pull of domination and resistance within society generally result in social services being contested terrains, similar conflicts exist within social work education. Indeed, conventional and progressive approaches often co-exist uneasily within the same college or university. By "progressive" I mean working towards an understanding of the root causes of social problems, along with taking actions to address these sources. This has also been called a radical approach to social work. By contrast, the conventional approaches reflect top-down influences and pressures and take up theories that attempt to legitimate social work as an efficient and credible profession in the eyes of the powers-that-be.

A prominent example of a conventional approach that originated in the United States about twenty years ago, and which still influences Canadian practice, is the ecological-systems theory. According to British scholar Malcolm Payne, this approach views individuals and their environments as being in constant interaction. Within this theory the "environment" of practice most often refers to a social environment that includes the social systems of family, community, and institutions such as the workplace, school, and social services. According to the theory, individuals "both change and are changed by the environment." Just as individuals are changing all the time, to a greater or lesser degree, so too the social environment and its systems are acknowledged to be constantly changing. In the context of these continuous changes individuals are viewed as seeking to develop their human potential. When individuals "are supported in this by the environment, reciprocal adaptation exists. Social problems (such as poverty, discrimination or stigma) pollute the social environment, reducing the possibility of reciprocal adaptation" (Payne 1997: 145).

Part of the social worker's job in addressing social problems, then, is to act as mediator to "strengthen the adaptive capacities" of both individuals and social environment (Germain and Gitterman 1980: 10). In this process workers are to encourage constructive responses from the various social systems, such as the family, school, or social services, that are interacting with service users. Conversely, social workers also encourage service users, as individuals, to formulate improved adaptive responses to their environments.

Despite its attractive ecological metaphor, this approach promises more than it delivers. By and large, the emphasis on adaptation means that, in practice, it is the service user who is typically expected to do the adapting. This is because of the substantial power imbalance between individuals and their social environments – an imbalance that is not effectively addressed by ecological-systems theory. At best, the application of this theory results in minor concessions from institutions and other social systems. The approach fails to address the deeper changes within individuals and institutions, the changes that are required to achieve social justice. In short the approach largely ignores questions of critical consciousness. For example, how are illegitimate privileges linked to unjust structures of power? What are the implications for social services and for helping social service users?

Diverging from the conventional approach to social work, progressive approaches are being articulated by a growing number of Canadian educators and practitioners, who criticize social services for dealing only with the symptoms of social problems (Baines 2007a; Lundy 2004; Mullaly 2010; Murray and Hick 2010; Sinclair, Hart, and Bruyere 2009). These critics, by recognizing various oppressive realities, have generated anti-oppressive approaches to social work education and practice. These anti-oppressive approaches seek to develop critical consciousness about harmful social relations and about how to reconstruct these relations in equitable ways. As Julie McMullin points out: "Social relations do not refer to interpersonal relations. Rather, they are structural and reflect power differences among groups of people. Examples of structured sets of social relations are class, age, gender, ethnic, and race relations" (McMullin 2004: 16).

ABORIGINAL CIRCLES IN THE CLASSROOM

As part of a shift away from a profession that was mainly White, Eurocentric, and rooted in the middle class, some schools of social work in Canada are emphasizing Indigenous approaches to helping and healing. These schools are located, for example, at the First Nations University of Canada (Saskatoon, Sask.), at Laurentian University (Sudbury, Ont.), and at Nicola Valley Institute of Technology (Merritt, B.C.). Wilfrid Laurier University (Kitchener, Ont.) is the first to offer a Master of Social Work degree specializing in Aboriginal Studies. Numerous other Canadian universities and colleges have taken initiatives to invite First Nations Elders and Aboriginal instructors to share their Indigenous knowledge as part of the social work curriculum.

Fyre Jean Graveline, a Métis (Cree) social work educator, describes how she introduced an Aboriginal perspective to social work students:

> In most Aboriginal Traditions, prior to ceremony, procedures are fol-
> lowed in order to prepare the mind and the body to be receptive to
> knowledge and insight, which may come from anywhere. Smudging,
> the use of burning herbs for purifying space and one another, has many
> effects on the individual and collective psyche. It serves as a demarca-
> tion of time, notifying everyone that "Circle Time" is beginning. It is a
> signal for the mind to be still and in present time; it provides everyone
> in the group with a shared embodied experience. As the sweet-smelling
> smoke encircles the area, it is easy to feel the calming presence of our
> plant sisters, entering and filling all of those present. (1998: 133)

Having participated in smudging at the opening of numerous circles
led by Indigenous teachers, and Elders, I can attest to this "calming
presence." It opens a pathway remarkably different from mainstream
teaching-learning. Graveline's approach also helps students to experience a changed consciousness about colonialism and racism. For
example, one of her students, reflecting on Aboriginal circles, wrote
about having "developed new ways of thinking aside from my white
middle class perspectives. Most of all I have gained an understanding
about my white privileges and how I can use my own voice to help
change society's racist attitudes and actions." An Indigenous student
in Graveline's class reported: "As class ended tonight, I reflected on
the wonderful experience that it was! I was so happy to finally be
able to express my Native identity as part of my being. It was the
first time that my Voice was actually being heard, not only by others
but by myself" (Graveline 1998: 73,124).

Social work educators are starting to learn from Indigenous
ways of helping – nudged along by Canadian social work conferences
that over the past decades have included an increasing number of
papers and workshops on Indigenous topics. One of the presenters at
these conferences, a respected Anishinaabe teacher, Elder Waubauno
Kwe (whose English name is Barbara Riley), has provided teachings
about the Anishnaabek Traditional Counselling Wheel:

> Unlike mainstream culture, spirituality is at the base of all (our) teach-
> ings and values. This view emphasizes balance, harmony and unity
> amongst all things – in particular within humankind and between each
> race. Aboriginal people are not an ethnocentric people. We are taught

respect, kindness, generosity and humility. Because of our holistic world view, we see the interdependency, inter-relatedness and inter-connectedness of all things among human beings, animals, plants, elements, and the universe. (Riley 1994: 8)

In these ways Indigenous knowledge is being introduced in universities, and it is also happening outside of Canada (Asmar and Page 2009; Nakata 2004; Cajete 1999; Indigenous Peoples Issues and Resources 2010).

Social work educator Cyndy Baskin of the Mi'kmaw Nation summarizes how Indigenous worldviews apply to social services:

> An Indigenous approach to social work and being a helper is one that seeks harmony and balance among individuals, the family and community. In using the teachings that have been given to Indigenous peoples, the worldviews strive to re-balance all aspects of an individual, family, community and society. This is done with the recognition that when the physical, emotional, psychological and spiritual aspects within an individual are out of balance, the rest of the family and community are also out of balance. This is one of the most fundamental teachings and is the basis for learning to work from an Indigenous worldview. (2009: 137)

Baskin notes that Western ways of helping may not fit with Indigenous world views because, for example, Western ways emphasize individualistic rather than community-based approaches. In addition, Anglo-American social work typically ignores spirituality, rather than placing it at the core of the helping process (2009:136). At the same time, it seems to me that those of us who are Anglo-American social workers can learn from Indigenous culture to develop a better balance between the individual and the community, just as our social work can be more attentive to spirituality. To the degree that we are open to learn from Indigenous culture, it also becomes important that we avoid stealing Indigenous knowledge. As Baskin warns: "Appropriation is the new tool of colonization. . . . To appropriate Indigenous spiritualities or other practices into western forms of social work without consultation of Indigenous people and without acknowledgement of Indigenous knowledge is no different than the theft of our land and resources centuries ago" (150).

Respect for culture is part of showing respect for people. This respect also applies to the diversity of individuals, groups, and communities that have been systemically silenced and oppressed. It is the basis of carrying out anti-oppressive social work.

ANTI-OPPRESSION PERSPECTIVES

Just as Indigenous approaches are posing fundamental challenges to mainstream social work education, similar kinds of challenges are offered by those of us who are anti-oppressive social work teachers, practitioners, and students. We oppose the systemic inequalities that create so much grief for social service users. Since social services and social work educational institutions are an integral part of the very society that has generated oppression in multiple ways, ranging from colonialism to ableism, it is no surprise that an abundance of systemic inequalities are to be found within social work education and practice.

In response to these system-created inequalities, feminist activists established social services that counter the assumption about expertise being the exclusive domain of professional helpers. Feminists used consciousness-raising approaches to redefine social work by helping service users recognize themselves as being experts in their own lives. Such redefinition integrates the personal and political aspects of social problems and their remedies. This approach retains the importance of relationships but believes that relationships flowing in hierarchical patterns (top-down) are as ineffectual as those based on assumptions of moral superiority. Feminist social workers have initiated ways of using this alternative form of practice. Helen Levine writes:

> Personal stress and distress are seen as a barometer, a kind of fever rating connected to the unequal and unhealthy structures, prescriptions and power relationships in women's lives. There is a rejection of the artificial split between internal feelings and external conditions of living and working, between human behaviour and structural context. A feminist approach to working with women involves weaving together personal and political issues as causes of and potential solutions to

women's struggles. Women's troubles are placed within, not outside their structural context. (1982: 200)

Feminist insights about linking personal and political issues have helped to move social work education in progressive directions (Campbell 2002). For example, in *Social Work and Social Justice: A Structural Approach to Practice*, Colleen Lundy emphasizes the importance for social work of taking a view of wider power relations:

> The challenge for social workers is to understand the broader political context and organization of society while responding directly to the immediate concern and needs of those who seek help. This type of analysis focuses on the socio-economic or structural context of individual problems and the power arrangements and the economic forces in society that create and maintain social conditions that generate stress, illness, deprivation, discrimination, and other forms of individual problems. (2004: 130)

To assist students to work towards social justice, social work educators taking an anti-oppressive or structural approach also emphasize the importance of diverse identities. Indeed, educator and clinician Maurice Moreau expanded the scope of radical social work in Canada by recognizing the diversity of oppressions and arguing that multiple oppressions were interwoven into the structures of systemic inequality. He warned about the futility of debates trying to show that any one particular oppression was more debilitating and therefore more central than another. Based on his research and practice, Moreau concluded, years ago, that ranking the various exploitative social divisions in a hierarchy of importance was not useful in combating the multiple sources of oppression: "Instead, the structural approach places alongside each other the divisions of class, gender, race, age, ability/disability and sexuality as the most significant social relations of advanced patriarchal capitalism" (Carniol 1992: 4).

In widening the focus to address a diversity of oppressions, social work educators are becoming more inclusive. For example, in teaching about ways to counter heterosexist privilege, Ryerson University professor George Bielmeier pointed out to me that there are at least four things that social work students should know:

1. Identify heterosexism and not homosexuality as the problem. 2. Understand issues confronting gays, lesbians, bisexuals and other sexual minorities. 3. Have knowledge of the history of discrimination against gays, lesbians, bisexuals and other sexual minorities. 4. Have knowledge of support services that are available in the community for gays, lesbians, bisexuals and other sexual minorities.

That kind of social work education also values experiential learning. Educator Tracy Swan, in documenting the responses of social work students to the disclosure of her lesbian identity, found that the self-disclosure was helpful to students not only in their thinking about heterosexism and homophobia but also in their personal and professional development. Swan's study affirms that challenging stereotypes can be discomforting. A student in Swan's class recalls her experience:

> There was an emotional and spiritual shift in me when you disclosed. It was one of those times when I became aware of personal work that I needed to do. I had to go home to process what the meaning of that shift was. One of the things I came to was that (and I hadn't realized to what degree) I had internalized heterosexism. The degree to which was of as much surprise to me as your disclosure. (Swan 2002: 13)

Educators committed to equity periodically critique the meaning of words and definitions that were originally intended to advance social justice. For example, queer activists Marion Brown, Brenda Richard, and Leighann Wichman point out:

> Homophobia has been widely defined as the irrational fear and hatred of people whose intimate relationships are with members of the same sex. The original intent of creating this definition was to remove the focus from the queer person and emphasize the illogical reaction aimed toward him or her. Lived experience and further analysis of this term over the years, however, has led to the critique that the suffix "phobia" suggests a psychosocial condition, which absolves the homophobic person of social responsibility and obscures the legitimization of homophobia throughout social processes. (2010: 158)

These activists also point out that describing the fear of queer persons as "irrational" ignores the history and contemporary context of how this fear has actually been "rationalized" by so-called scientific evidence (when medical science defined homosexuality as pathology) and by punitive biblical dogma and hurtful cultural customs. To put it another way, using the term homo-"phobia" results in "diverting attention from the systemic discrimination toward queer persons that the culture of homophobia perpetuates" (159) because it narrows the focus to individualized thoughts, feelings, and behaviour as the sources of heterosexist abuses.

This kind of periodic review of language is part of education for the delivery of non-oppressive social services. Certain definitions that at first sight appear anti-oppressive become, upon further reflection, questionable based on our lived experience. Another good example is our prevailing belief that educators striving for equity have a responsibility to develop a safe space in the classroom. Drawing on her research, social work educator Betty Barrett notes that safety in the classroom is commonly viewed as the instructor's responsibility so that students will feel comfortable enough to express themselves without fear of judgment (2009: 5).

Barrett cautions us that a goal emphasizing student comfort may inhibit critical discussions focused on oppressive beliefs that have been expressed in the classroom. Such critical discussions are often uncomfortable. In asking "whether the safe space classroom is conducive to (or counter) to the development of students as critical thinkers," Barrett also focuses on power differentials:

> Students who belong to racially, socially, or economically marginalized groups live in a world which is inherently unsafe – a world where racialization, sexism, ableism, classism, and heteronormativity pose genuine threats to their psychological, social, material, and physical well being. To contend that the classroom can be a safe space for these students, when the world outside the doors of the classroom is not, is not only unrealistic, it is dangerous. (2009: 8)

Are we offering safety, then, mainly to students who already have the privilege of safety and self-expression, at the expense of students who experience marginalization? Barrett is not advocating for a classroom climate that is closed-minded, intimidating, and opinionated. On the contrary, she suggests that we strive to create civility in the classroom rather than aim for the illusion of safety. About the link between civility and expressions of respect in the classroom, Barrett explains: *"I think expressions of respect are a necessary condition for the classroom to be constructed as civil space. The pedagogy literature is pointing to a movement towards the term 'civility' in the classroom which appears to have emerged out of a broader discussion about the role of higher education to socialize students into the norms of civil society."*

As I reflect on how to achieve genuine respect in the classroom, it seems to me that instructors need to be partisan. By partisan, I don't mean that instructors should single out and embarrass a student who makes, for example, a heterosexist slur. I do mean that in such a situation instructors should point out that heterosexist abuses and stereotypes are not only extremely common, but are also "natural," in the sense that they result from media and cultural messages that continue to flood us with images, based on sexual orientation, that devalue people. At such teachable moments, educators can deconstruct society's harmful narratives; and we can then invite students to brainstorm about how things would be different in a society that accords full human rights to queer persons. What would be different in how we think, feel, and act towards lesbians, gay, bisexual, and transgendered people? What would be different in our laws, policies, and institutional practices? What could each of us do to contribute to such a transformation?

Through such classroom discussions, educators would not be able to create a totally safe space – which, as Barrett notes, is an unrealistic goal – but they would be helping to create a classroom that would be less unsafe for members of various oppressed populations. Less oppressive classrooms will in turn contribute to social change initiatives for reducing oppression outside the classroom, as a small but significant step towards the elimination of all forms of oppression everywhere.

Part of an anti-oppressive curriculum is anti-racist education in social work, which at times is mistakenly equated to "anti-oppressive" education. With such an equation comes a risk of sacrificing the critical edge that an explicit anti-racist education provides. Narda

Razack and Donna Jeffery warn that in social work, "Core analyses of race have been quickly cloaked under the rhetoric of anti-oppression, diversity, cross-cultural approaches, and multiculturalism" (2002: 259). A weakened focus on racism is dangerous, they say, because "unearthing the technologies of domination imbedded in social work knowledge and practice requires that Whiteness be explored and demystified as an ideology that is oppressive and false" (265).

Roopchand Seebaran, professor emeritus at the University of British Columbia's Social Work and Family Studies, recommends a number of ways of maintaining a focus on anti-racism in social work education:

> A focus on the school community as a target of intervention and learning about anti-racism; dealing with incidents of racism in the school and the field agencies; collaboration with local communities in joint research initiatives; the development of curriculum and teaching materials related to anti-racism practice; and a focus on experiential learning. (2003: 313; see also Jeffery 2009)

Educational initiatives into the multiple sources of oppression are proceeding, then, even if in an uneven fashion. Our understanding of the intersecting areas of privilege and oppression is evolving, along with our growing recognition about the complexities of teaching this approach (Murphy et al. 2009; Wehbi 2009). Mullaly cautions against mechanically adding up the various relevant oppressions. Given that "different forms of oppression intersect with each other," he says, "these intersections contain oppressive effects themselves." Social service workers will have to "recognize that not all members of a particular oppressed group will experience oppression in the same way or with the same severity or intensity. Just as there is heterogeneity between groups of oppressed people there is also heterogeneity within each oppressed group" (2010: 203).

Social work educator Wendy Hulko, in writing about the intersection of oppressions, recommends:

As educators we need to help students appreciate that they can be both oppressors and the oppressed at the same time. . . . This may be a particularly powerful experience for students who may be aware of their marginalized social status because of their Aboriginal ancestry or ethno-cultural background, for example, yet may not have considered how their social-class position has afforded them more opportunities than members of their communities. (2009: 52–53)

Although the precise definition of anti-oppressive practice is still a "work-in-progress," the value of recognizing and resisting oppression has been clearly recognized. For example, schools of social work across Canada are expected to follow the Accreditation Standards of the Canadian Association for Social Work Education (2008). Those standards state: "The curriculum shall ensure that students achieve transferable analysis and practice skills pertaining to the origins and manifestations of social injustices in Canada, and the multiple and intersecting bases of oppression, domination and exploitation" (17–18). But the move to adopt the right words does not in itself necessarily bring appropriate action. Those words are a helpful first step – not insignificant in moving towards social progress – but significant change comes through implementation.

Numerous educators and practitioners are indeed taking steps to implement this approach (Clarke 2003: 247–63). As it is, social workers have tended to follow two divergent and at times conflicting approaches. (See Table 1, which attempts to clear off some of the conceptual fog that impedes understanding – although actual practice rarely fits into neat boxes.) Always, in both teaching and practice we need to keep in mind the sharp differences that exist between conventional and progressive social work.

Social workers use a set of skills in areas such as assessment and empathy. How workers interpret and apply these skills will depend on whether they are committed to progressive values that include equity and social justice as a priority within their practice, or whether they hold a conventional approach that insists upon professional social workers remaining non-political. It is not unusual for social service providers to hear: "Political change should be left to elected politicians; it's not part of social work."

Table 1
Social Work Skills in Social Services

Social workers applying:	Assessment skills	Empathy skills	Reframing skills
Conventional ecological and systems perspectives	Use systems theory and ecological life model: (1) to explain dysfunctional interactions among different systems (e.g., individual, familial, communal, and formal systems); (2) to explore imbalances between individuals and their environments; (3) to identify areas for reciprocal adaptation by individuals and other systems, to optimize human well-being.	Communicate an understanding and appreciation of the client's feelings and subjective experience (as part of developing trust within a professional relationship). Use this skill in working directly with individuals, as well as with individuals in families, groups and communities. Develop anticipatory empathy by tuning in, as part of preparing to work with specific client systems.	Aim to reduce clients' sense of hopelessness by suggesting new, more hopeful ways of viewing the situation. Congratulate clients for achievements that are ignored or devalued by others. Invite clients to identify unrecognized strengths within themselves and in their interactions with other systems, to help empower alternative, positive, and more hopeful client responses.
Structural and anti-oppressive and critical perspectives	Use structural, critical and liberation narratives: (1) to focus on systemic oppression and oppressive narratives (e.g., colonialism, patriarchal capitalism, racism, heterosexism, ableism, ageism) as harmful to the service user's well-being and as creating illegitimate privileges; (2) to identify immediate survival needs; (3) to explore short-term and long-term goals for emancipation.	Communicate efforts to learn about and appreciate the service user's feelings, stories and meanings (as part of trust evolving within a non-elitist professional relationship). Widen focus to include emancipatory empathy: i.e., dialogue about subjective and systemic barriers faced by others similarly oppressed, and about the courage to name and to overcome such barriers.	Aim to reduce self-blame by co-investigating with service users: (1) external and internalized oppression; (2) external and internalized illegitimate privilege, due to unjustified power over others. Explore new, more hopeful narratives and ways of understanding/ acting, in light of social justice inspirations and initiatives and solidarities.

By contrast, social workers who apply structural/anti-oppressive /critical perspectives are practising a different, better version of professionalism by assisting service users to recognize how the personal and political dimensions of their lives are interwoven (Carniol 2005a: 391–92). Using progressive perspectives, we deliver social services that build on insights from, for example, feminist, anti-racist, and anti-colonial ways of helping people. As progressive service providers we use analysis based on various social sciences, including class analysis, that draws upon the lessons of history. A progressive approach insists on the inclusion of voices from anti-poverty groups, queer communities, (dis)Ability activists, and others claiming their rightful place within society. We therefore challenge colonialism, racism, heterosexism, patriarchy, capitalism, ableism, ageism, and all forms of systemic oppressions that run roughshod over people's dignity.

FUTURE TRENDS?

Within social work education, then, a number of initiatives and approaches are beginning to challenge the multiple sources of illegitimate privilege. Yet many people in Canada still believe that social programs are a waste of taxpayers' money, and more specifically that social assistance programs are given more money than they need. We have all been influenced by these messages. Indeed, some social work students have indicated that they believe these messages are true, and that "a few minor adjustments will fix the system." Many students are in for a mixture of shock and confusion when they confront the actual conditions in social services.

"I went to the welfare office. The waiting room smelled of urine. It was smoke-filled with no ventilation, a small room holding eighty people. The walls were kicked in. There were cigarette butts everywhere. I had to go through locked doors to get to the offices and I felt like I was a prisoner. When I asked about the locks, they told me the staff was threatened – if clients can't get their cheques some go berserk. . . . There was no dignity there. The place made you feel like scum. It was as if the whole structure was accepting it. When I talked about it with other stu-

dents, they were concerned – but only for the staff. These students were not upset by it and were accepting of it. They were too caught up in carrying out their role in handing out cheques."

Social work's official aspirations of achieving social justice – and practical ideas for bringing this about – still have a long way to go even within social work education. Elizabeth Radian of Red Deer College, Alberta, told me about some challenges:

"One disturbing trend is the debate about recognizing community college diplomas as a valid credential for social work practice. I believe there is room in social work for all levels of credentials, ranging from social work diplomas to graduate social work degrees. To try and exclude college diplomas in social work ignores social work values that are oriented to inclusion.

"Another disturbing trend is to rely primarily on grades when accepting students into undergraduate social work programs. While grades do suggest a level of academic ability, they do not necessarily indicate a potential for sound and ethical social work practice. My concern is that we may be excluding many good future social workers, who may not have had the same opportunity to excel academically but have rich personal experiences that would be an asset for social work."

In her doctoral research on social action, Radian found that most of the social workers she interviewed were social activists before becoming involved in social work studies. Most of them had also either *"experienced marginalization themselves, and/or had wonderful social activists as role models."* Often, and *"somewhat surprisingly,"* she noted, *"these activist role models were grandmothers who were active in their communities."* Their own experiences and these role models had influenced them *"to engage in social action focused on eliminating social injustices, even at the risk of jeopardizing their employment status."*

Social work educators do not work in a vacuum. They are part of larger colleges or universities that are designed on a model of top-down power flow, and that are encouraged to view education as preparation for labour markets that fit into the hierarchies within business and government organizations. Given the depth and persistence of racialized, gendered, colonial, and other unequal social relations in the wider society, it is not surprising that university hierarchies today are also permeated by these systemic inequalities. In some cases, universities have honestly acknowledged these shortcomings (Taskforce on Anti-Racism at Ryerson 2010). Only time will tell whether university administrators will follow through on their promises to remedy the problems.

Those of us who spend time in universities cannot help but notice the increasing corporate influence, ranging from preoccupations with "the bottom line" to shifts in language so that students increasingly become "customers." In addition, like other academics, social work educators learn about a host of rules and policies governing such areas as grading criteria, course design, and examination protocols. The expectations to conform to these rules apply generally to post-secondary education, as do the pressures on professors to spend more time on research (and therefore less time with students). As a consequence the social relations between professors and students are often experienced as impersonal and alienating. These negative student experiences are aggravated by inadequate government funding, which results in larger class sizes, among other things. Furthermore, realizing the importance of good grades to their academic success, students have a strong incentive to feed back what professors want to hear.

More specific to professional training are the field-work courses that place students in social agencies as part of the curriculum. Students are assessed not only on how well they relate to clients, but also on how well they respect the agency's mandate (and its limitations) and fit into the agency's work. Assessments of student performance are still too often rooted in those social work theories that aim at "helping" service users adjust to unjust conditions. Not that students are expected to issue directives for service users to follow. The process is far more subtle. Students are encouraged to ask about what service users want, to empathize with their problems, to explain what the agency can or cannot do, and to offer help only on terms acceptable to the particular agency. In this way students learn to replicate professional roles that provide help based on the requirements and needs of social service organizations.

Students are taught that by acquiring social work competency via technical skills, they will be capable of enhancing service users' interpersonal relationships and enriching their interactions with specific systems within our society. As a result, many students develop an excessive faith in their own professional privilege and in the power of their emerging technical expertise to overcome problems that are essentially of a political and structural nature.

The sense of professional elitism is partly created, and often nourished, by the educational experience of social work students. It springs as well from history and from the prevailing political, economic, and social relationships. Finally, in professional practice, these power relationships are often firmly buttressed by many of the institutions and agencies that end up employing the graduates of social work education.

5 SOCIAL WORKERS: ON THE FRONT LINE

I think my empathy level had gone. The continuous problem
after problem after problem and seeing nothing done and it
coming back to me. It was so repetitious you almost lose your
feelings with it . . . which is really sad for me because I'm
quite a compassionate person innately . . . and I hated that
part of it.

— a social worker in Saskatchewan,
documented by Patti Cram

If both social service workers and their sense of altruism are
under pressure, it is clear that as much – or more – of this pressure comes from above, from government policies, state managers, and corporate leaders, as from below, from service users and
their allies. Part of the pressure too has come from the unprecedented expansion of social work in the post–World War II era.

Membership in the Canadian professional social work associations grew from a total of 600 in 1940 to 3,000 in 1966 to over
24,000 in 2009 (Canadian Association of Social Workers 2009; Ordre
professionnel des travailleurs sociaux du Québec 2009). This tendency towards professional expansion has not proceeded without
challenge. Governments and business leaders wanting to justify cutbacks have accused social workers of drowning clients with an over-
abundance of services. Social workers have been accused of doing
too much for troubled families, thereby weakening the family as an
institution.

Part of the pressure on social workers also comes from the role they adopt and practise – as professionals. The average salary levels for social workers are modest, but, after all, money isn't everything. Social work's capacity to make professional judgments, to channel service users along one path instead of another, to offer advice to decision-makers about what social programs should be doing: these are elements of professional power. At the same time social workers, like some other professionals, such as nurses and teachers, are not a power unto themselves. Social work also exists as part of larger institutions, which are in turn shaped by larger forces.

Most social workers are employees of social agencies (also known as social services), which are in turn influenced directly or indirectly by state authorities, and the practice of those agencies is an integral function of the overall system. In Canada the state includes a wide range of government commissions, departments, and agencies supposedly organized for the purpose of enhancing the public's general welfare – by which is meant our social as well as economic well-being. One way of promoting these goals is the deployment of social workers within social agencies, both within and outside government.

WHERE SOCIAL WORKERS WORK

Social workers are employed in a number of different social services. They may work in the *voluntary sector* for agencies such as the YWCA /YMCA, Elizabeth Fry Society, or John Howard Society. The terms "voluntary sector" and "voluntary agency" are sometimes misunderstood to mean that the services are provided by volunteers. But while volunteers do offer services in some of these agencies, the volunteers typically supplement the services that are delivered by paid social service providers. The agencies in this sector are designated "voluntary" because they are governed by voluntary boards of directors made up of individuals who receive no direct remuneration for their activities on the boards. These boards in turn hire service providers, including social workers, to carry out all or part of their programs.

Sometimes the voluntary agencies are established by religious or cultural/ethnic groups that raise their own funds to finance, for example, the Aboriginal Family Support Services, Catholic Family Services, United Chinese Community Enrichment Services Society, Salvation Army, Jewish Home for the Aged, or Jamaican Canadian Association's Settlement Services for New Immigrants. Many of the agencies in the voluntary sector receive funding from donations collected through local charity appeals, such as the United Way. It is mainly from within this sector that much of social work evolved into a profession during the early part of the twentieth century. Increasingly, however, these agencies are also obtaining supplementary funding from governments and are thus becoming more and more influenced by government policies and organization.

The voluntary sector is part of what in Quebec has for a number of years been widely called the "social economy." In collaboration with other Quebec social service analysts, Yves Vaillancourt defines the social economy as "a vast array of enterprises and initiatives, mostly from the non-profit sector, including advocacy groups, voluntary organizations, other community-based organizations as well as cooperatives." These organizations are oriented towards innovations in networking and democratic practice, based on "values of solidarity, autonomy, reciprocity and self-determination" (Vaillancourt et al. 2004: 314, 315).

Throughout Canada a small but growing number of social workers also work in private practice, running their own offices much as lawyers do, with clients paying fees for service. Social workers are also employed in the quasi-government sector, in settings that have voluntary boards and are partially autonomous as organizational structures, but are at the same time governed by legislation and regulations, and have funding that originates from the state. Hospitals and public schools, which often employ social workers, fit into this category.

Perhaps the best-known example of the quasi-government sector is the Children's Aid Society in Ontario, in which social workers obtain their authority from provincial legislation. Each Ontario Children's Aid Society, in different locales throughout the province, has its own volunteer board of directors, which establishes further policies and standards for social workers to follow. (Most provinces maintain child welfare agencies within the public sector – that is, operated directly as part of the government.)

Still, undoubtedly the largest single area of social work is in the form of direct employment in the government or *public sector*. Government agencies carry out services that are often statutory; their tasks and the decisions they make are specified by government regulations and policies. An example is social assistance, better known as "welfare" – or "workfare." These programs provide for the payment of limited amounts of money to people who have little or no financial resources. Social service providers assess the needs of applicants for assistance and decide whether they qualify based on the agency's regulations and policies. Increasingly automated and depersonalized, today these programs allow less and less time for counselling and job-training projects. A greater emphasis on the applicants finding jobs is reflected in the names associated with welfare programs. For example, Ontario's social assistance program seems to have copied "Alberta Works" with "Ontario Works." In Quebec the program is administered by the "Ministère de l'Emploi . . ." Nova Scotia, Manitoba, and British Columbia use almost the same labels: "Employment Support and Income Assistance," "Employment and Income Assistance," and "BC Employment and Assistance Programs."

Although social work has often been equated with welfare or public assistance, social workers are employed in numerous other agencies within the public sector. A partial list includes probation services within juvenile and adult correctional branches, alcohol detox centres, mental health clinics and psychiatric services, outreach programs for homeless youth, and long-term care for people with (dis)Abilities (Canadian Association of Social Workers 2010a).

It is not unusual for the different categories of client populations to receive help from both the public and voluntary sectors. For instance:

> Social workers have been working with people with (dis)Abilities on numerous fronts, from community development to establishing advocacy groups, community living centres, and, overall, a place for (dis)Abled persons within society. They also help families secure the services and resources necessary to combat barriers associated with

accessibility and accommodation, and engage in individual work recognizing the person with the (dis)Ability as the expert on his or her
own life and abilities. (MacDonald and Friars 2010: 141–42)

Most social work textbooks present social work from an urban
perspective – they assume that service users are total strangers to service providers, and that numerous specialized services are in place.
While most Canadians live in cities, social services are also available
in rural settings in which people have bonds to the land, and where
services are sparse. In rural settings, there may well be only one
social worker in the entire community, with a supervisor in a distant
location. As a worker in the Maritimes, for instance, Rosemary Clews
has found that living in a small community means that you tend to
get to know people before they come to you, which results in relationships based on greater authenticity (Clews, Randall, and Furlong
2005). For that reason some social service providers prefer working
in rural settings.

How People Become Social Service Users

The needs that bring someone to a social work agency – or bring an
agency to someone – are many and complex. The problems can
range from violence against women to poverty, child abuse to alcoholism, drug addiction to marital strife, or conflicts in the paid workplace or at school.

If you have had a serious illness that prevents you from return-
ing to your job, you might have to seek out a social agency to get
financial help or advice. An AIDS patient in a hospital or a student
having difficulty might be referred to the hospital's social worker or
the school district's social work counsellor. You could get a visit
from a social worker if you are a parent and someone (a neighbour,
teacher, or doctor, perhaps) suspects you have violently abused your
child and reports you to a child welfare agency. If you have been
convicted of a crime the court might order you to report to a probation officer, who may be a social worker. The *official* message to
social service users is: we are here to help you (Canadian Association of Social Workers 2010b). The more subtle message is: we are

here to help you with *your* personal or interpersonal problems, as if the problem arose entirely within yourself. Frequently hidden from view is how these "problems" are caused or aggravated by systemic inequalities.

If you are experiencing severe interpersonal problems (within your family, for instance), you might seek out social work counselling. That would probably bring you to a social agency in the voluntary sector. Or you might find yourself going to a private practitioner's office.

There is a marked contrast between someone voluntarily seeking help – say, with an addiction – and an involuntary situation in which a court compels someone to receive social services. A rough rule of thumb is that involuntary social services are provided by government agencies, whereas the voluntary sector tends to offer services that clients are free to accept, reject, or approach on their own initiative. Thus the term "voluntary" applies to more than the social agency's board. It can also apply to the level of choice involved when someone accepts, or doesn't accept, the social worker's services. To the degree that a person's choice is reduced, state authorities move in with their own definitions and solutions.

The Challenge of Social Work

Depending on the agency and the service population, most social workers offer access to financial and other resources and provide various types of counselling. Providing access to resources might include helping someone get access to subsidized housing, searching out a decent nursing home for an ailing parent, or seeing that a child with a (dis)Ability is able to get to the right summer camp.

One of the hallmarks of social work competency is the ability of workers to establish effective interpersonal relationships with clients. This requires that the worker attempts to enter the world of the client psychologically, to create enough of a sense of empathy and establish sufficient rapport to elicit a description of the problem as seen by the client.

All of this, needless to say, is not an easy task, and certainly it can be argued that it is impossible for a social worker to ever fully understand the world of the client. This difficulty is compounded when a social worker's identity (culture, class, gender) is different from that of the client. Around the beginning of the 1970s, a Nova Scotia group including Black social work researchers reported:

> It is obvious that many clients experience some discomfort in accepting help from a Black professional social worker. We have been questioned about our qualifications and many clients seem shocked (and sometimes a little skeptical!) to learn that we have graduate training from an accredited School of Social Work. We are also frequently asked about our place of birth. We are both Nova Scotian Blacks – from East Preston and Halifax respectively. Many whites, especially those from the lower socio-economic groups, find it difficult to believe that a Black Nova Scotian could have attained such a position. They find it equally hard to be in a position of having to receive help from one. (Bernard, Lucas-White, and Moore 1981: 23)

Some years later the same authors stated, somewhat sadly: "As we reflect on our experience of the past 10 years, we realize that little has changed. We must still work twice as hard to build our credibility, to prove our competence, to attain whatever goal we have in sight, and then to hold on to it" (Bernard, Lucas-White, and Moore 1993: 267).

As Black activists Wanda Thomas Bernard and Veronika Marsman point out, the Association of Black Social Workers was established decades earlier to intervene in a social service system "that was not responsive to the problems and concerns of African Nova Scotians" (2010: 194). The Association's participants became concerned when child welfare agencies said they could not find Black foster and adoption homes for Black and biracial children: "The experience of racism and cultural alienation was an everyday occurrence for most of these children at home, at school, and in the neighbourhood" (196). In response the Association worked to implement an Africentric set of principles based on "an African worldview that includes harmony, collectivity, and non-materialistic qualities of people; connects people culturally, historically, spiritually, and with community; and views the experiences of African people as key movers of their own liberation" (193). These principles, sometimes implicit, have guided the Association of Black Social Workers over its thirty-year history. During that time it has pushed for the province to recruit and retain Black foster and adoption homes, and advocated for and succeeded in improving provincial family legislation. It has also run youth programs, including lessons in African Nova Scotian and world history and sessions in dealing with racism and handling conflict. This project is a case of social workers not limiting themselves to counselling, but becoming involved in public education, policy/program advocacy, and community development.

People often feel ashamed or confused about the stressful situations that have prompted them to contact social services, whether it is alcoholism or unemployment or violence in the home. Social workers therefore need to be skilled in asking the appropriate questions, in observing, listening to, and focusing on painful topics. In theory we try hard to be non-judgmental, to refrain from criticizing or blaming service users for their situations. In actual practice we too often focus primarily on our own views, our own preconceptions, our own definitions of problems, and our own sense of what is "normal."

For example, considerable heterosexism exists among many social work educators, students, and professionals who accept the prevailing systemic stereotypes that dehumanize lesbians, gays, bisexuals, trans, and other sexualities. The implications of this tendency for practice are serious because people with different sexual orientations do use social services. For example, children may be concerned about their sexual identities, or lesbian mothers may be seeking custody of their children. How will service providers treat people of all sexual orientations with respect if social service agencies continue to privilege heterosexuality as the only form of "normal" sexuality?

When gay and lesbian older adults go to counselling for issues such as excessive use of alcohol, they might encounter a situation described by a website dedicated to alcohol issues and older people: "In many cases, counselors were not fully sympathetic to, or even knowledgeable about, being gay. Some would even go so far as attempting to 'cure' a client's homosexuality, falsely believing that their gayness was the root of their excessive use of alcohol" (Aging in

Canada 2010). Attempts to "cure" people whose sexualities differ from heterosexuality have a shameful history. It includes the Nazi Germany period, when gays, lesbians, and other queer persons were arrested and forced into concentration camps, where they had to wear an identifying triangle sewn onto their clothes and were experimented upon by doctors who used various injections to search for a "cure" for their sexuality. Today in North America, though not at the point of the gun, "curing" is being pushed by religious fanatics who use fundamentalist dogma to pressure lesbian, gay, bisexual, and transgendered people to get into "treatment programs." Though at best well-meaning, such "treatment programs" represent a further level of insults and oppression under the guise of "help."

The contested terrain of social services includes the push and pull of heterosexist norms versus respect and support for human rights, including rights for sexual diversity. That kind of respect and support can be found most consistently within agencies that are specifically oriented to the needs of queer people and that adhere to queer-positive values (O'Neill 2006: 335, 342). Although coming "out of the closet" is by no means an easy step in our society – it can alienate friends, family, workplace supervisors, and service providers alike – research has shown that being out has its advantages in relationships with health and social service providers. A group of researchers based in Montreal, Toronto, and Halifax (Brotman et al. 2007) looked into the experiences that caregivers of gay and lesbian older adults had with health and social services. They found that caregivers who were themselves gay or lesbian – and were out – tended to have a sense of entitlement and assurance of their own rights and as a result usually felt the most comfortable advocating for the rights of care receivers to full and equal access to services. They stressed the need to empower older adults and their caregivers as well as the need to develop explicitly gay- and lesbian-friendly services or safe spaces for those caregivers and care receivers who might still be "in the closet." Among other things, employees at all levels need to have proper training "so that they provide a warm and welcoming environment" (501).

Such welcoming environments in health and social service organizations need to include bisexuals, transgendered, and other queer people who face immense difficulties when coming out because of the conventional view of being "either male or female," attracted to "either male or female." In contrast to these binary prescriptions, the more fluid identities experienced – for example, by bisexual people – are complex, and require social services that avoid slotting people into fixed categories. Someone who reflected about her own counselling experience recalled:

> A person could be straight for a number of years and then live in the gay lifestyle for a while and then return to the straight lifestyle as I have. Would said person be bisexual or straight? I tend to value the romantic and spiritual connection that I have with someone over the body parts they possess. I believe this is what makes me truly bisexual. If I like you I don't care what is in your pants. I will work with whatever is there. However, a counselor at my local GLBT community centre has diagnosed me as straight after asking me a bunch of questions about my likes/dislikes. (Madison 2009)

Service providers can be most helpful when they are open to the lived experiences of the people they are working with, but all too often such openness is undermined by a culture of prejudices against certain identities. Considering the case of transgendered children, for example, Gerald Mallon cautions service providers: "Just as it is important that transgendered children are not mislabeled as gay or lesbian, although they frequently self-label as such prior to coming to a full understanding of their transgendered nature, it is also important that gay and lesbian children are not mislabeled as transgendered." He points out that in contrast to gay and lesbian children, who ultimately accept their gender while being attracted to others of that same gender, transgendered children have a consistent dissatisfaction with the gender they were born into; they find themselves identifying with a different gender (1999: 60, 59).

When trans adolescents defy gender expectations, they often face a backlash from family and peers, and especially at school. According to one analyst, this situation can lead to "intra-psychic problems and behavior such as depression, low self-esteem, substance abuse/hormonal abuse and self-mutilation, compounded by additional factors such as running away from/being kicked out of one's home, homelessness, prostitution, dropping out of school and unemployment" (Burgess 1999: 58). Although this comment was made over ten years ago, the heterosexism that spawns mistreatment of queer populations continues unabated, as suggested by a 2009 U.S. survey of transgendered students' experiences at school: "90% of transgender students heard negative remarks about someone's gender expression sometimes, often, or frequently in school . . . and also reported little intervention on the part of school personnel when such language was used" (Trans Youth Family Allies 2009: x).

Prejudices are generally deeply entrenched. This is true not just in the case of sexual orientation but also regarding Indigenous peoples, women, people with (dis)Abilities, people living in poverty, and other groups that experience systemic injustices. It is therefore not surprising that when social service providers recognize prejudices in an agency's policies and practices, and then try to change them, life in the agency can become difficult. Feminist social work researcher Lisa Barnoff cited a service provider who found that, despite "working their butts off for the whole organization," workers were targeted for dismissal after they were told they were "too radical" or "too loud or obnoxious" (2002: 227). Barnoff also recounted how an employee in a feminist social agency experienced her work as highly pressurized because, in the service provider's words: "The work that women do as a whole is constantly being minimized, put down, under a microscope, always criticized. You're functioning within a framework where you're always trying merely to survive and constantly to legitimate your very existence" (2002: 296).

So too, negative attitudes about prisoners from correctional institutions result in social agencies struggling to help their clients. An executive director of a Halifax employment project set up to aid prisoners from federal penitentiaries found herself working on a shoestring budget that had been cut back: *"If a prisoner isn't able to find a job after release from prison, what happens? He can go on welfare but many are too proud, so where can they get money to pay for food and rent? Crime becomes very tempting and the next thing you know, they're back in prison. Our society spends a lot on punishment, jails and the like but little on positive help."*

Workers in government welfare or workfare departments face a different challenge. They often carry caseloads of individuals and families that number in the hundreds, which leads to a different kind of struggle to survive. One of them told me: *"From a service point of view, I don't even have time to listen to clients. In one recent month my total caseload was over 215 cases! I burnt out last August. During one hour then I had as many as five cases of evictions to deal with. It got to the point that emotionally I gave as little as I could to each client. Of course clients realize it and get resentful."*

Government social services tend to establish rigid policies. Indeed, as social service employees in these settings, they know they are expected to follow bureaucratic rules and policies. These rules in turn often place them at odds with service users. Supervisors are usually nearby to remind social workers about the agency's expectations. A social worker in a public assistance agency in British Columbia said: *"As a social worker, you know it's impossible for a family to stay within the food budget. But you find your supervisor is putting pressure on you – to put pressure on the client to keep within the budget."*

The benign-sounding official goal of "helping people" opens the door, then, to demands by state authorities, via social workers, that social service users accept, conform, and adjust to the rules. This puts a squeeze on service users. It also creates discomfort for many service providers who try to maintain a sense of personal accountability, of decency and respect for others, as distinct from the requirements of the agency. As one social worker put it:

"The rates for welfare are so inadequate that you'll often find a mother, father, and child all living in one room in a rundown hotel; it's the only place they can afford because the rent elsewhere is too high for them. The place has no cooking facilities, so they eat by going to a greasy restaurant and buying things at 7–11 and corner stores. You find mothers trying to toilet-train their child where there's no toilet in the room, so they have to go down the hall – to a toilet shared by several tenants."

Knowing that as a professional helper you are not really going to be helping clients get on their feet produces a sense of demoralization – primarily among service users but also among social workers. After all their training, social workers discover that while their social services do provide some help to clients, at best they can barely scratch the surface of the problem. Within agencies, tensions can build and explode. A social worker at a social assistance office in Vancouver told me this story:

"This rather large fellow comes up to the receptionist. You can see he's not drunk – he's stoned. He's about six-foot-five, I mean, he's big! And he asks for something. He's told by the receptionist he can get it from his own welfare office. He asks for some coins for the bus. The receptionist, an eighteen-year-old woman, starts to look in her purse to give him some change.

"I was in the middle of a conversation with another social worker who overhears the client asking for change. She stops talking with me, turns around and tells the receptionist, 'No! Don't give it to him!' Well, that big fellow – he just blew! He swung both arms across the reception desk – the phone, papers all went flying all over the place.

"As if this isn't enough, this social worker now tells him that I walk that distance once each day! I felt the social worker should have just shut up. I was looking around the waiting room to see if anyone else was looking to join a fight. You can get a few clients all getting angry and you can get into some pretty heavy duty stuff! Luckily everybody was still calm.

"I wanted to defuse the situation fast. So I tried to change the tone by saying, 'Actually, I don't walk once, I do it twice.' This fellow did see the humour of it, but added his own by hissing at me – Thhhaatssss your tough luck!!!' Meanwhile somebody had called the police. He turns to leave but before going, he points his finger at the social worker and says, 'YOU'RE FUCKIN' DEAD!!!' She wilts. He walks out."

When abused and mistreated people explode in anger – either individually or as a total community – we may react with fear or with self-righteous indignation about "their overreaction." But, as anti-racist educator Paul Kivel wrote in his classic book, *Uprooting Racism: How White People Can Work for Racial Justice* (1996: 107), "Rather than attacking them for their anger, we need to ask ourselves how many layers of complacency, ignorance, collusion, privilege and misinformation have we put into place for it to take so much outrage to get our attention?"

A glimpse from a social worker employed by a social assistance agency reveals more reasons for outrage.

"During the time I'm supposed to write up my clients' files, my day is interrupted by walk-ins – homeless families with nowhere to go, crises of all sorts, phone calls from anxious clients I haven't had time to call for two or three months. There've been some days I haven't gotten near my files. So I have to do it on my own time. It's difficult, some husbands get angry when you bring work home. But if you don't your supervisor is on your case. The clients are angry too because they haven't received their cheques because you haven't had time to write up their file.

"We're talking basics here. It could be a family that's been evicted with five or six children; there's no groceries so they're hostile. That's why our casework is critical to their well-being. Yet the demands go beyond our energy or time. Talk of pressure!"

The barriers faced by service users often originate in the dysfunctional ways in which social services are organized, as well as in the unhelpful policies that social workers are expected to follow. In agencies designed to protect children from abuse and neglect, government policies have been established with little or no input from social workers on the front lines. An example is the expectation that social workers will carry out certain types of risk assessment procedures when there is suspicion of child abuse or neglect. These procedures are rigid. They prescribe when supervisors must be consulted and rely on extensive checklists and computer data entry. This type of risk assessment has been criticized by numerous practitioners, educators, and policy analysts. Social work educators/researchers Marilyn Callahan and Karen Swift found that as a result of heavy emphasis on this type of risk assessment, child welfare workers spend much of their time doing investigations and out-of-home placement of children. That leaves "little room left for supportive efforts by social workers trained to provide these [support] services," Callahan and Swift say. "We need to restore balance" (2006: 214; see also Parada 2009). Put another way, policing by social workers has become far more important than helping to support families, and far more important than working to prevent child abuse and child neglect.

Canada's national social work association documented similar findings about the failures of child welfare agencies. It warned that child welfare services in many provinces are failing to implement the officially established purpose or mandate for which they received government funds: "In many jurisdictions legal mandates are not being met, client needs are not being met, and social workers are not meeting the ethical requirements of their profession." The Association of Social Workers concluded that the service organizations were "more interested in saving money than [in] providing quality service to children and families." It saw "limited resources both within the agency and in the broader community . . . as a chronic impediment to good practice." As for the social service employees, "a lack of recognition and support" had left many of them "feeling victimized, helpless, isolated and disenchanted" (Canadian Association of Social Workers 2003: 10, 12; La Rose 2009: 234).

These limitations in child welfare services are even more aggravated for Indigenous youth. Susan Strega and Sohki Aski Esquao speak from first-hand experience. As children, both of them were clients of child welfare. Both of them eventually became social work educators who wrote the book *Walking This Path Together*, which focuses on anti-racist and anti-oppressive child welfare practices. From their research, they conclude: "Present efforts to support Indigenous child welfare agencies are doomed to failure because the policy context is one of continuing to control and monitor Indigenous populations through funding formulas that privilege child protection over prevention, family preservation and support" (2009: 22).

Professor Cyndy Baskin, of Mi'kmaw and Irish descent, identifies a major problem with the delivery of social services to Indigenous people generally, not just to youth: "One of the main problems when non-Indigenous helpers work with Indigenous adults is that they overlook the Indigenous person's culturally held beliefs and values, instead using an approach to social work they assume to be universal" (2009: 136).

Yet barriers to decolonization do not go away even when social services are delivered by First Nations people. Yvonne Howse of the Cree Nation teaches social work at the First Nations University of Canada in Saskatoon. She explains:

"For me the issue is – we still have that slave mentality which says Western theory is superior to First Nations traditional methodologies. Aboriginal clinical practices are generally not honoured. For example, many Indian child welfare agencies depend on Western consultants to develop their programs. These consultants bring with them Western theory and methodologies based on their ten to twenty years of practice within mainstream child welfare agencies. That is one example where they say: 'This is how we do it' – and we say: 'Yes, Master.' Our colonized mind makes us believe that anything other than Western practice is inferior. Therefore our traditional methodologies are not used in most Aboriginal child welfare agencies.

"Within our communities, there still are healthy families that practise traditional First Nations methodologies. It is our belief that the family will sustain us through these difficulty times. It is the family that is important for future generations. That is why our traditional practices are so important.

"We don't want our children to be apprehended. But there are no dollars for prevention work – very few dollars or services to support these families. I've come to the conclusion that we have to speak up about these issues. Silence is oppression. But we need to do more than just talk. Until our own Aboriginal social agencies honour our own First Nations traditional methodologies and practices, our communities will not become healthy – and nothing will change."

For social service providers committed to change, the challenge that Yvonne Howse articulates is enormous given the strong structural barriers, and their related privileges, that stand in the way. Sometimes those barriers are broken down and innovative programs begin to help people. But all too often in a variety of areas ranging from work with women who have been abused to youth who are unemployed, the innovations become unravelled due to enforced limitations on the scope of social programs. A social worker in the Maritimes, for instance, had established a program for school dropouts who were in conflict with their families and the law. The program consisted of building solid relationships with the youths and taking them out to work on fishing boats.

"*After a couple of weeks the kid would return home and the mother would tell me – 'My son looks great! I don't recognize him! He's got a tan, developed a bit of muscle, the lines under his eyes are gone, the tension is gone, he looks great!'*

"*But it was all a mirage. Those changes meant nothing . . . nothing! Because these kids went right back into their old situations, there were no other choices. We had a temporary program and when it was gone, the kids were left with nothing, no jobs, just like before.*"

Is it any wonder that some professionals drop out? It begins with a yearning to escape, as one social worker told me: "*The other day I heard about someone on the west coast, he built himself a small house on top of a tree, overlooking the ocean. I really like that idea, imagine letting the wind come and swaying you in that tree and just being free. I might go and find a tree like that . . .*"

DEALING WITH CHALLENGES: TINY MIRACLES

The evidence is overwhelming: the challenges facing social service providers are enormous. They include the consequences of annual cuts in many social programs such as social housing, child-care programs, income supports, and various social services. These program cuts, as a result of tax cuts demanded by Canada's privileged elites, have restricted the capacity of social workers to provide effective help. While some people exit from work in the social services, surprisingly most social workers and most social service workers remain. In light of the incredible challenges, what on earth would motivate anyone to stay within such a beleaguered environment?

From my years of experience and from listening to many seasoned social workers, I believe the answers have to do with certain values about life. I'm not sure if we as human beings are "hardwired" by a need to see people treated decently, or whether we are nurtured into these values at an early age by caring people, or whether there exists some combination of these two or other factors. But I do know that such values run deep within many, if not most, people. From observed behaviour I can also clearly see that these caring values are stronger in some people and weaker in others. But contrary to postmodernists who claim that there are no universal truths, my observations point to this human quality of caring about others being present across different cultures, different nations, and different time spans. Granted, too often this quality is suppressed or otherwise blocked. Nevertheless, caring about others seems to be a universal quality that is expressed differently by people from different cultures, different parts of our planet, and different time periods.

This core value of caring provides us with the resilience to "hang in there" to deliver social services even under the most adverse conditions. It is also my observation that experienced helpers are not naïve. We experience the constraints and the frustrations of the work. We recognize that even when our social services successfully help service users, we still live in a society infused by harmful expectations, behaviour, and attitudes that flow from systemic forms of privilege and oppression. Neither the helpers nor the people being helped escape the constant barrage of commercials and other mainstream messages that encourage us to escape into consumerism and its preoccupations with self-indulgent satisfactions.

Yet such negative pulls fail to dissuade most of us from delivering the best social services possible under the circumstances. Social services enable us to "stand with" people who experience exclusion and to oppose unjust structures. As we stand in solidarity with individuals, families, and communities that have experienced systemic disempowerment, we try along with many others to make a difference. Sometimes the results are small miracles.

At times and despite all odds, social services offer opportunities for good practice, along with dedicated workers who deliver it. Sandra, a mental health social worker in Alberta, is an example:

"When I first met Melissa (not her name) she kept her head down so far I couldn't even see her eyes. I could hardly hear her voice, she was so extremely soft-spoken. She had been severely abused as a child. When

we first met, she was living in a shack with her son – no running water, no conveniences, and the roof leaked.

"*In developing a therapeutic relationship with her, I remember giving her many choices. I suggested she could write down some of her experiences of abuse. I said she could burn what she had written and I'd never see it. Or she could write about her experience, then give it to me, and I could read it in her presence. Or she could write it up, leave it with me, and I'd read it before our next meeting when I'd give her feedback. She decided on the last option. So that's what we did. She wrote, left it with me, I read it. Then we met for me to give her feedback. We did this for three months.*

"*When we talked, I validated her pain, helped her to identify her inner strengths, and affirmed these strengths. I started to see progress. I pointed it out to her. She needed encouragement, which I gave her. She started to take charge of her life. We worked on her goals, such as finding better housing. At the end of three months I felt she was on her way to developing the confidence she needed.*

"*About four or five years later, Melissa came in to talk again. She was now talking face to face. I could see her eyes easily. She was much more confident. She was excited to tell me that she'd gone back to school – upgrading – and was now a university student working on her degree. She was living in her own place, a decent place. I could tell she was on her way! That was very satisfying for me. I felt I'd helped her turn things around. I'm Aboriginal like she is. Our communities have such problems: it felt good to help someone from our communities. My husband is Aboriginal too, and I couldn't do this work without his support.*"

The pockets of social services across the country that do contain effective forms of practice typically include the service users in direct decision-making. In central Alberta, clients of mental health services in nine communities carried out leadership roles in conducting a survey of service needs. According to Elizabeth Radian of Red Deer College, "*The clients were effectively involved in the project from beginning to end – from the initial planning to the presentation of the project at a conference.*"

Over the years the value of professionals sharing their power with service users has been increasingly recognized as a component of good practice (Carniol 1992: 8; Carniol 2005a: 391–92; George, Coleman, and Barnoff 2007: 11–13; Mullaly 2010: 240; Peters 2010: 48–50). For example, one research project of the early 1990s – *Empowerment II: Snapshots of the Structural Approach in Action* – surveyed the work of thirty-one progressive social service employees who had graduated from Ottawa's Carleton University. In reflecting on their practice, various workers made comments such as: *you need to feel comfortable not being in control . . . you need to be able to join the client versus treat the client . . . you have to involve yourself in challenging the agency without shafting yourself in the process . . . you have to have an acute awareness of society and politics and see this and from there pull the skills.*" The authors of the report concluded that, based on this sample, "There is a shared feeling that social analysis is key to assessment and for many this informs the use of skill" (Frosst 1993: 106, 119, 120, 126).

My own observations and experiences over the years suggest that when social work skills are informed by progressive social work perspectives, the outcomes are far more empowering to service users compared to the same skills being applied by social workers using conventional perspectives. (See Table 2, which shows the contrast in ways in which social workers apply skills, depending on whether they are able to share power with service users and link their work with progressive social movements.)

In addition to the well-known communication and advocacy skills, the growing dangers of fundamentalism within numerous faith communities mean that social workers are increasingly being expected to be sensitive to the difference between legitimate spirituality and harmful beliefs masquerading as spiritual. As social work educators, administrators, policy developers, and service providers, we take up the task of supporting progressive religious practitioners who act in opposition to harmful and oppressive religious practices within polarized faith communities. In a different context, when we strive to become allies to Indigenous communities, we need to be able to respond respectfully to Indigenous ceremonies and to the spiritual content that is so central to Indigenous cultural traditions.

In applying a progressive perspective, Catrina Brown, a feminist

Table 2
Social Work Skills in Social Services

Social workers applying:	Communication skills (e.g., listening, exploring, focusing, clarifying, encouraging)	Spiritual sensitivity skills	Advocacy skills
Conventional ecological and systems perspectives	Listen. Explore ways in which clients and their environments can better adapt to each other. Focus on services / resources, while affirming client strengths. Explore stress reduction among clients, families, and other systems. Offer respect and support client self-determination. Mediate / guide client systems in their problem-solving and solutions-finding.	Validate religious / spiritual pluralism. Support spirituality by clients as a strength to cope with stress (e.g., life transitions, crises caused by painful losses). Honour / appeal to spiritual / religious values of compassion and charity within / across diverse communities to encourage more generous help for people in need.	Work at convincing formal and informal systems to better meet client needs, by urging greater charity for many disadvantaged populations. Be active with others in lobbying larger systems for better policies, co-ordination, integration, and delivery of social services. Seek support from private, public, and charitable sectors, for additional resources to alleviate social problems.
Structural and anti-oppressive and critical perspectives	Listen. Explore ways in which clients may be victims and survivors of oppression. Focus on services / resources, while affirming people's strengths. Model power-sharing with service users. Unmask illegitimate privilege. Support narratives pointing to personal / political transformation away from multiple oppressive practices, and towards equity.	Validate religious / spiritual pluralism. Oppose religious narratives and practices that are oppressive. Learn about and honour spirituality rooted in diverse cultures, including its role in Indigenous people's helping and healing. Find spiritual / religious inspiration for progressive personal and social change within / across diverse communities.	Act with others, including service users, to challenge oppressive narratives / practices. Defend human rights (e.g., decent jobs, incomes, universal social programs). Organize grassroots power upward to resist harmful policies / decisions / processes / structures. Become allies with social movements, locally and globally, for personal, familial, political, economic, and spiritual emancipation.

educator at Dalhousie University in Halifax, writes about how women with alcohol-use problems may develop subjective under-standings based on a disease model that define themselves as having deficits and disorders. She gives an example of a client whose stories about herself described her as being "no good." Brown notes that, with help, the client reassessed her stories and was able to develop new stories or re-author her stories in a way that challenged her self-perception about being "no good." This client had revealed to the counsellor that during her childhood and adolescence she had been sexually, physically, and emotionally abused. The client's stories about herself suggested that she had no right to feel anger or pain. Brown discusses challenging the client to explore how her drinking "actually makes sense in the oppressive and painful context in which she has lived. This exploration encourages self-compassion and acknowledges that she is entitled to her anger and pain. . . . The goal of feminist therapy is not to discover the real self underneath pain and oppression. Instead, feminist therapy focuses on building less oppressive or preferred stories of the self" (2007: 142).

Based on her research, Ryerson professor Purnima George demon-strates how some social service providers are managing to give priority to the needs of service users. One worker said:

> We work with youth and hire them. We provide support and bring in resources, connect them to others if we can't help them directly. It's very empowering. They see themselves as a part of something better. They have ownership – plan, implement, evaluate programs. They walk away with skills that they can use in any area of life. They walk away feeling a sense of hope which they didn't have.

Another said: "I network, attend their meetings, and participate in rallies. I get out and get involved with allies as I know I can't do it alone. I have good relations with workers of other coalitions and I make use of my good relations to help solve the problems of my ser-vice users" (George 2003: 40, 36; Burrill and Peters 2010).

Despite these encouraging examples of good practice, the over-all picture is one of social workers responding to a greater number of services users with greater problems. No wonder some social workers – who try their best to carry out good practice – become bitter:

"It's rather irksome when social workers are criticized, say by people outside the department, and yet management never tries to defend the quality of commitment by social workers. Meanwhile, we're sweating it out . . ."

To challenge such negative experiences, and to push for an expansion of services that provide effective help, we need to take a closer look at the management of social services. Why do social service managers, more often than not, collude with oppressive expectations? As we develop a critical analysis of social service bureaucracies and as we also listen to the voices of service users and service providers, we will be better able not only to resist oppressive pressures, but also to align our practice with emancipatory approaches in the delivery of social services.

6 MANAGING SOCIAL SERVICES: FROM TOP TO BOTTOM

> There's no latitude to do anything creative or new. None. We just do what the form says. I've been in this job a long time. I know what would be really helpful to the client but we're not allowed to do it. We just follow the form and the clients don't get help and we might as well all just work in a widget factory specializing in how to make society worse. It really stinks.
>
> — a Canadian social service worker,
> documented by Donna Baines

As an acting director of a social development agency in Montreal a number of years ago, I was concerned about the inadequacies I saw in welfare services. When I let it be known to my co-workers and superiors that I intended to speak out on these problems, to go on public record, I received quiet yet clear messages about my "short-sightedness." Furthermore, when I joined welfare recipients who were staging a sit-in at a social assistance office to protest low welfare rates, many members of the agency's board of directors saw my attitude as "unbecoming of a professional."

After that, had I wanted, for instance, to become executive director of the agency, there would probably have been sufficient opposition from the board to block the appointment. Most of the board members came from the upper echelons of society, from high positions in business and the professions. They believed in general that things were being taken care of efficiently and properly, to the basic good of all concerned. The few problems they saw were limited to "abuses" of the system, usually emanating from the service user end of things. Sometimes they saw problems as being caused by "bad apples" or malcontents: social workers who were not trying hard enough to make things work; or service users who were not trying hard enough to pull themselves up by their bootstraps. At the most, they thought, the problems called for some careful, judicious, and "realistic" mediating.

These boards typically see the issues from the perspective of a White, male, dominant class that at best patronizes disadvantaged populations, at worst works to protect its own interests and to prevent any inkling of significant change. The top-down flow of power – via gender, cultural and other prejudices, and hierarchy – has a major impact on the maintenance of inequalities inside the social services.

THE STRATIFICATION OF SOCIAL SERVICES

Social services are stratified in much the same ways as our government and business bureaucracies are. Among the reasons given for such a stratification are greater efficiency and accountability of the organization – a rationale widely accepted by the public, including the professionals within our social services. We also assume that those at the peak of the social agency's pyramid are the most qualified and competent. According to this theory, a measure of a person's competence in social work is an ability to rise up the career ladder.

Social service workers are taught that the current structures of authority are necessary and desirable, with little consideration of whether alternative, more democratic organizational structures might better serve service users. This is how a social work textbook defends bureaucratic hierarchies: "Someone has to be in charge, especially in large complex organizations, and there have to be clear lines of authority. Having a set of rules is also essential in the interests of fairness, stability and efficiency." The same textbook also notes, "Along with being accountable to ourselves, our clients, our profession, and our community, we are first and foremost accountable to our employers" (Pillari 2002: 93, 91). The loyalty to a hierarchy is offered as a "natural" condition, and the descriptions of the hierarchies tend to ignore their contested nature and downplay the aspect of social control embedded in organizational structure. Similar social service hierarchies exist in the voluntary and government sectors; the main difference is that in the volunteer sector, social work managers or executive directors are accountable to voluntary boards of directors rather than to a government minister.

Another difference is size: a voluntary agency is usually smaller than a government agency. Voluntary boards, however, are influential in giving direction to social agencies and in promoting their credibility in the eyes of major funders. As in the public sector, social service executives strive to provide their operation with effective management. This includes financial management and supervision of either departments or front-line staff, depending on the size of the agency.

While social work executives in the voluntary sector are in strategic positions to speak out about the effects of unjust social conditions upon service users, they usually don't. It is not so much that they are told to keep quiet. There is a much more subtle process at work as administrators learn that boards prefer a smooth operation, free from community or public controversy.

Boards are usually also active in a monitoring role. As part of this role, the board has the power to hire and fire its executive director. Social work executives, therefore, realize that the board plays a crucial part not only in relation to funding bodies but also in evaluating the executive's performance. In other words, there is not only the question of the agency's financial position but also the matter of the executive's professional survival as manager of the agency.

The top-down flow of power becomes, among other things, a channel for punitive actions against social service providers, leading to a profound sense of alienation. This was illustrated some years back in Alberta after a series of scandals involving foster parents abusing foster children. In response the provincial government decided that social service providers in its child protection divisions must visit each foster child and each family on their caseloads once a month. As one of the social workers told me, at first glance it sounded like *an improvement over just letting situations drift endlessly.* But the worker added:

"Now comes the catch: with 90 or 120 children on your caseload, plus all the paperwork, tell me how it's possible to carry out this policy? It can't work! It's impossible! Now if something blows and a child is harmed, the managers can say, 'We have a policy, why aren't the workers carrying it out?' A classic case of blaming the victim! You answer, 'But there aren't enough hours in the day,' and they can't hear that. The managers will pass down the blame to the supervisors – why can't you manage your units? And the supervisors will yell at the line workers – why can't you manage your cases?"

If the constant demand for acquiescence does not wear us down, and if we retain our abhorrence of arbitrary power, promotions create other hazards. A supervisor can easily become divorced from front-line colleagues and client realities. Supervisors begin to represent management. A level of mistrust towards managers develops among front-line workers, and the managers react to that mistrust. According to a supervisor in a welfare office: *"You find you now have two levels, your previous colleagues who are still line workers and your new colleagues who are also supervisors. You find yourself talking to other supervisors about 'they' at the line level, as if somehow 'they' were not quite as wise as you supervisors. 'They don't know.'"*

Gradually the separation becomes solidified. As a supervisor you attend certain meetings, you have access to information and decisions – an access that the line staff does not have. Misunderstandings can easily develop, with line staff suspecting or knowing that you are holding back information. Many supervisors do try to be open with front-line workers, and some succeed. But such openness occurs despite the agency hierarchy, not because of it. More often workers who move into management find themselves jumping to the defence of the system.

In class terms, just as the interests of managers in business corporations become identified with the owners, managers of social agencies (and most of their consultants) identify primarily with the interests of those in control of the social service delivery system. In both cases, front-line employees emerge as a separate group, subordinate and subservient to the power of the managerial group.

Agency hierarchies may reward certain competencies, but their patterns of promotions and salaries indicate that other priorities are also being served: that the management of social work is governed by the larger, structural relationships of society as a whole. For instance, in a study of the salaries of male and female social workers, social work educator Gail Kenyon collected data from over one thousand social workers across Canada and found that on average male social workers earned 22 per cent more than female social workers did (2003: 195).

Given the patriarchal structure of our society, that outcome is not surprising, even when it applies to social work, long considered a female profession. As well, because the most basic caring for and nurturing of others have long been defined as women's work – whether paid or unpaid, whether in the home, community, or workplace – male social workers benefit by being favoured over women for managerial positions. Yet Kenyon's study (2003: 197, 200) found that, even when women reached administrative positions, the gender income gap remained high, with men earning 21 per cent more than women. Kenyon's findings led her to issue a challenge to social work: "Is it logical to ask the profession to combat discrimination and the lack of opportunity for women in our practice when we cannot or will not address these issues within the profession?"

Aboriginal leaders are making their own attempts to move towards equity, turning a public spotlight on the assimilationist legacy of colonialism. Reflecting on her experiences as a social worker, Barbara Waterfall, a Métis Anishinaabe-Kwe, points to the depth of Eurocentric narratives and their impact on practice:

> Social workers failed to recognize the effects of residential schools on Native families, or other debilitating consequences of oppression. They did not respond fairly or appropriately [which would have meant] encouraging the teaching of Native traditional child care practice. . . . Traditionally, Native child rearing was valued as a sacred responsibility. Children were nurtured in a community sense of belonging. Children were encouraged to develop mastery of skills that were needed for survival. Punishment was not a concept that was used traditionally by Native peoples. Rather, techniques such as modeling, group influence, and positive expectations were employed. (2006: 232, 229)

Colonialism, racism, and other forms of institutionalized privilege continue to permeate Canadian public and private sectors, and, as Waterfall notes, there are implications for social services. Also affected by racism are racialized Black, Afro-Canadians, and people of different ethno-racial backgrounds. These groups were the focus of a study by social work researchers Kevin Gosine and Gordon Pon (2010), who looked at the experiences of racialized child protection workers in the Toronto area. Many of the participants expressed concerns around systemic racial discrimination in the promotion and advancement of service providers within these agencies. In addition, based on the experience of the racialized child protection workers in this study, Gosine and Pon found that services to racialized service users often felt the impact of negative stereotypes combined with little appreciation of cultural differences. These researchers noted that racialized workers in these agencies had to "contend with white-normed and middle class oriented policies, tools, and practices which often prevented them from meeting the unique needs of racialized service users" (2010: Abstract, 1).

This kind of study clearly documents the gaps between official mission statements (usually inclusive) and actual practices – and illustrates the need to place progressive change on the agenda of social service organizations as well as of social work educational programs. A good beginning would be to invite members of disempowered communities and their community organizations to meet with the organization's decision-makers to discuss at least a couple of questions. How could these gaps between official goals and actual practices be reduced or eliminated? How might hiring outcomes, promotion practices, and service delivery become consistent with anti-racism approaches?

These questions could prove threatening to managers who are not committed to equity – which is why some social service managers are not always willing to meet with representatives from the populations that their agency has been set up to serve. When progressive workers continue to raise the pertinent issues at staff meetings or elsewhere, managers will at times orchestrate a backlash that includes disapproval, anger, or personalized attacks. When I have been involved in these kind of situations – that is, in pressing for change – I have found that members of disempowered communities have become supporters and allies. They help me and others weather the storm of backlash. After the dust has settled, the organizations may well be ready to implement new, more progressive, and inclusive practices.

My experiences have also confirmed that the anti-colonialism and anti-racism approaches offer doorways into a host of other systemic inequalities ranging from heterosexism to class privilege – because focusing on any one oppression can open the way to addressing all of them. Indeed, one of the goals of anti-oppression practice is to widen the scope of practice to include the entire cluster of systemic inequalities.

The Bottom Line

Business management approaches – conventionally reputed to be a means of maximizing efficiency – are not limited to the commercial enterprises of the private sector. Non-profit and public-sector agencies also adopt "business plans" and apply business management approaches in their operations, in order to manage workplace speedups, cutbacks, and heavy workloads. Demoralizing working conditions and unsatisfactory services tend to be the result.

Examining data obtained from over eighty front-line social service workers in Alberta, British Columbia, and Nova Scotia, Donna Baines found: "Full-time, permanent, unionized jobs in the social services sector are being rapidly replaced by part-time, contract, on-call and other forms of temporary insecure work" (2007c: 90). Intensified managerial control has meant not only that risk assessment comes under closer scrutiny, but also that "intake forms, case notes and even supervision are increasingly standardized, often taking the form of step-by-step 'best practice' flow sheets, computer case management packages and check box forms in which the interactions among layers in the social work endeavour are tightly scripted" (Baines 2007c: 90–91; La Rose 2009). As she documented the flow of social service work being "sped up and readily assumed by part-time, temporary and contract employees," Baines noted that the result is a de-skilling of social work (2007c: 91). As a result, "Most workers felt that new forms of management have closed down ways in which employees used to have input into the priorities and organization of their agencies" (88–89). Baines and others criticize these new forms of management for creating new barriers to social services and for lowering the quality of services that in turn increase the hardships experienced by social service users.

Subordination to directives issued from above creates a sense of powerlessness and frustration. A social worker student documented what happened soon after a social worker started working for a child protection office in Western Canada: "I can remember after about three days of work one of the senior workers was looking something up on the computer and she said 'That stupid fucking bitch.' She was talking about a client. I was horrified that anyone would talk about anyone, especially a client, like that." In her university social work courses this new worker had learned about the "modelling of equality" – about oppression and ethics and about placing the emphasis on human rights and social justice. She had been "brought up to be respectful," she said. But not long after going on the job she found herself looking at the clients in much the same way as her senior colleague was doing. "Within a month," she said, "I was talking the same. . . . That's how I was talking" (Cram 2004: 101).

The imbalance in power created by the top-down business management approach has much to do with this outcome. As a service provider in a voluntary agency serving youth and families puts it, "*The person who supervises you clinically is the one who hires you, is the one who fires you, is the one who disciplines you, and is the one who overrules you.*"

Given the squeeze on so many front-line service providers, it appears that the job of social work is being granted professional status only in a symbolic sense. In this context anyone attempting to do advocacy work finds that it is not an easy route to follow. For instance, Deena Ladd works with a Toronto community-based worker advocacy centre that offers support to short-term contract workers – "*people who are in precarious jobs – they have low pay, no union, and incredible inse-*

curity." She "*noticed that advocacy is a dirty word in most social agencies, not just in agencies working with employment programs.*" A good part of the reason for this, she says, is "fear." The agencies receive funding from various levels of government, and their administrators are afraid that if they speak out they will lose their funding.

As part of her job Ladd does workshops with well-established social agencies that provide employment services, including job developers, job placement people, and employment resources centres. The funding bodies expect these agencies to find a certain number of jobs a year for their clients, and if they don't find that certain number of jobs, the funding will be cut accordingly in the following year. "*So this puts pressure on these agencies to meet their quota, which in turn puts pressure on front-line staff to find whatever job they can for the people they work with – often people of colour who are immigrants and refugees.*"

What happens as a result is that, with the quotas constantly in mind, the social agencies send workers out to take jobs that have both low pay and inadequate working conditions. When a worker comes back from one of those jobs and asks for help because she or he hasn't been paid as promised by the employer, the agency offers little or no support. "*Front-line staff are discouraged from doing advocacy,*" Ladd says. "*The message from government is not usually explicitly stated at their various training sessions, but you're still left with strong hints that they see low-paid, temporary part-time jobs as inevitable, as the way of the future. So just get used to it.*" This lowering of expectations, lowering of labour costs, Ladd concludes, is "*in line with what corporate globalization is doing in so many places.*"

Although social work professional associations can discipline their own members for unethical conduct, these associations have no clout when it comes to protecting any social service provider who wants to do advocacy work. The day-to-day control over practice is not exercised by the profession but rather by a combination of agency and social service managers, beholden to funders who have their own agenda. During this process, front-line workers experience increasing disempowerment – which is in itself a reason for welcoming labour unions into this field of work.

LABOUR UNIONS AND SOCIAL WORK

Labour unions are formed not just because workers need better pay and want to overcome horrendous working conditions. They are also formed because workers are fed up with arbitrary, dictatorial managers – and this is as true in non-profit social services as it is in the private, for-profit corporations. Even though the playing field remains highly uneven because of the larger legal, political, and economic authority vested in management, unions give voice and limited protection to people who otherwise would be worse off. They represent a practical way of contesting the one-way flow of power from above.

Most social service providers are employed at workplaces that have been unionized. The advantage of being part of a larger union is that members benefit from the strength of the larger group and its collective agreements. Unionization, especially in the public sector, has raised salaries for social service workers, although the government often rolls back these gains through contracting out or by demanding wage concessions. For example, the federal government offered to pay the John Howard Society (a non-profit, voluntary agency) to carry out parole work that would otherwise be done by the better paid federal parole service. While such moves are ostensibly to save money, they effectively undermine the job security and improved working conditions that federal parole officers have won through collective agreements.

It is well known that, historically, labour unions have struggled for better working conditions and pay. Perhaps less well known are the efforts by the labour movement to urge governments to introduce social programs such as old age pensions, unemployment insurance, and medicare. These social programs would not have been established if organized labour had not pressed for them through the political arena. During periods when these programs come under attack it is, again, the labour movement, along with others, that organizes opposition to the cutbacks.

Although unions strive to be among the most democratic of our institutions – with rank and file participation a visible priority on convention floors or in meeting halls – feminists and diversity advocates have criticized them for being not only White, male-dominated, heterosexist organizations but also preoccupied with product rather than process, and for avoiding the needs of women and people having diverse sexual/cultural/ethnic identities. From my experience with labour unions, I have noticed that pressure from unionized people of colour and from sexual diversity activists has led to the development of human rights programs within unions. The message delivered is that racism and heterosexism weaken the union movement. Similarly, feminist activists are making unions more responsive to gender equality.

Confronted – directly and indirectly – by the women's movement, the union movement has become more active in pushing for equal pay for work of equal value, child care, maternity leave, pensions for older women, paid child-care leave, sexual harassment, and other concerns initiated by women.

Yet the reality is that for many front-line social workers, women as well as men, union involvement means one more meeting, on their own time, on top of an already overloaded schedule. For the majority of front-line workers, who are women, the obstacles are even steeper because many are burdened with the double workload of employment and child care. At the same time, for those workers who do become active with their unions the benefits are clear. According to social worker and union leader Karen McNama: *"Unions are important for front-line social workers because they serve as a protection against abuses by managers. By 'abuses' I mean the long hours we are made to work; the heaviness of the caseload and I don't just mean numbers. Unions allow us an opportunity to have a voice, to disagree with management without getting hit with 'insubordination.'"*

In recent decades, as a result of quiet, worldwide organizing by business leaders, most governments have become either openly or discreetly hostile to social programs. As a result in Canada, funding cuts were implemented at the federal, provincial, and municipal levels, with severe negative impacts on social services. Community worker and social work educator Tara La Rose documented the consequences for social workers in a child welfare agency in Toronto, where she found that service cuts resulted in the remaining workers agonizing over unreasonably high caseloads.

In addition, new funding rules led to such a high volume of computer entries and paperwork that one service provider recalled being pushed into what felt like a factory system, with high staff turnover. "We were treated as just disposable. You leave and someone else comes. The worker would just become a cog" (La Rose 2009: 234). Small wonder that many workers felt "devalued, deskilled and disrespected" (233).

These social workers belonged to the Canadian Union of Public Employees (CUPE), which provided what the employees needed: a forum that made it possible for them to reach a consensus about their workload. They wanted management to put a limit or cap on the number of cases that front-line workers were expected to respond to. Management refused, causing social workers to go on strike. La Rose (2009: 241–42) reports:

> After six and a half weeks of running the agency without direct-service staff, under widespread pressure from the public as well as the union, the employer conceded to the workers demands. Caseload caps and workload language became a part of the collective agreement. Where workload disputes could not be settled through internal grievance procedures, the Ministry of Labour would make a ruling on the issue through binding arbitration. Never before had a quantitative limit been set in a child welfare sector contract.

Aside from the victory of having the employer accept limits on workload, La Rose points out that the strike gave workers a greater sense of personal empowerment, less alienation at the workplace, and more confidence in their abilities. They could question management directives with greater confidence; and they noticed how some managers were more responsive to their concerns. In this example, union activity also fostered the type of peer support so important for effective social work.

At other times unions have helped to augment the resources needed by clients. An experienced social worker, Pam Chapman, told me about her work at an emergency shelter in a dilapidated, stuffy building that was understaffed and overcrowded – full of babies crying and mothers yelling. Staff had been continuously asking management to address the building's conditions, but nothing had changed.

"Fortunately the union did make a difference. The union steward got all the staff together and invited us to document the problems as well as our suggestions for solving these problems. Besides the overcrowding issue, we wanted a children's program in the shelter. The union called a meeting with the shelter's management and demanded action. Soon after, the children's program was established and other conditions improved as well."

While unions provide opportunities for empowerment and have both improved working conditions and contributed to better social programs, they do not speak with one voice. Aside from differences such as whether a union represents workers in the public sector or industrial sectors, and the particular affiliation of the organization, unions also have differences in perspectives. The contested terrain of conflicts and contradictions that operate at the larger societal levels also exist within the labour movement itself, just as they do within social services. The more conservative unionists tend to restrict union activity to a focus on the working conditions of their own members; the more progressive unionists recognize the importance of focusing on the wider systemic issues that arise in a system dominated by private corporations wanting to expand their privilege. That is why progressive unionists engage in continuous campaigns of political education that at times influence the larger labour movement to adopt emancipatory directions.

For students, educators, and workers, the labour movement's emphasis on solidarity and collective action in general casts the role of social workers into a broader emancipatory context. It encourages both reflection and analysis of wider issues and the formation of important links with other movements and other workers.

PRIVATIZATION OF SOCIAL SERVICES

In many countries of the Western World during the decades following the Second World War unions slowly gained strength and social safety nets expanded, placing both developments on a collision course with the goals of the corporate sector. Aside from focusing on government deficits and tax cuts, corporate leaders came up with two other notable schemes to remake the world in their own image: contracting out and privatization.

Contracting out – in other words, employing a workforce that is outside of the collective agreement signed by managers and unions – means that, once again, workers become shut out from negotiating the terms of their employment. The employers become "free" to pay lower wages than those required under union contracts.

Privatization means the transfer of public services to the private sector, where they become for-profit operations. The growth of privatization in recent decades stems from business leaders, their think tanks, and their special interest groups lobbying government to move institutions such as prisons, hospitals, public schools, universities, and social services away from the public sector and into the private sector. This shift means changing these services from non-profit into profit-making enterprises.

At least two types of non-commercial services are targeted for privatization. One type consists of services that have until now been directly carried out by government; in other words, services that are considered part of the public sector, such as prisons. A second type consists of services that until now have been provided by organizations outside of the public sector, but funded by government. An example would be home care or personal care services (for example, house cleaning, bathing) for frail older adults in their homes (Neysmith 2006: 403). In both instances governments are changing the process of allocation of funds. In the past, the accountability involved annual reviews by government managers focusing on service performance, costs, and other organizational factors.

Governments are now introducing competitive bidding for both types of services – that is, those operated by government and those operating outside of government. Of course, only the services that are deemed capable of generating profits are being targeted for privatization. The successful bidder gets awarded the contract to run the service, be it a prison or home care. All participants in competitive bidding must supply the government with detailed plans specifying operational programs and associated costs over the life of the proposed contract. The steps and resources required in preparing viable, clear, and comprehensive plans are very expensive. While politicians proclaim that the bidding process is open to all, very few non-profit social agencies have the resources to invest in such a process. Private corporations have another advantage: they typically calculate their costs based on a non-unionized, low-paid workforce. As a result they can often underbid the not-for-profit agencies, which pay salaries that are not particularly high but are generally higher than those paid by private corporations.

As international trade agreements between Canada, the United States, and other countries are being fine-tuned, it is not difficult to imagine global corporations using their power to obtain terms in these agreements that would open the floodgates to business ventures headquartered outside of Canada to bid on such contracts.

Prior to competitive bidding being introduced, friendly competition existed among voluntary sector social agencies. Voluntary boards would team up with their staff of service providers to position themselves favourably with funders, trying to show how they were meeting the service users' needs. Now, given the shortage of public funds, governments seem to be shifting away from an emphasis on the service users' well-being and quietly asking: What is the cheapest way of delivering the service? Yet the cheapest service can also be the least effective service, as is frequently evidenced by periodic scandals at for-profit nursing homes (Welsh 2004: A1).

Where not-for-profit agencies, such as home-care services for frail senior adults, are required to engage in competitive bidding against business firms, the pressure mounts for all workers to adopt an impersonal factory model for social services. An administrator of a non-profit long-term-care agency comments on the effects of privatization:

"For the client, there's no choice. A hospital will tell them, 'You go home NOW: we'll give you home care at the level we decide.' Clients come out quicker and sicker from hospitals, which increases the responsibilities of home-care workers. And by metering out maximum levels of service, staff is pressured, for example – when giving a bath to a client,

to be in and out of the client's home in half an hour, little time for talk, little sense of humanity – off they rush to the next client. That, plus the government's efforts to compress wages, leads to less job satisfaction, and will over time lead to bigger job turnover – with less continuity of service for clients. While all this is happening we see non-acute clients being squeezed out of services they used to receive, and having to rely on the private market."

Reductions in public services due to tax cuts are resulting in the growth of for-profit social services that are not limited to serving older adults or people recovering from serious illnesses. This shift is occurring in a number of different service areas, such as those responding to people with (dis)Abilities. Peter Dunn points out (2006: 419): "As federal standards have diminished and provinces further fragment the service delivery system by downloading responsibilities and reducing supports, private for-profit disability agencies have emerged. Many of these agencies are concerned with profits rather than with the empowerment of consumers."

The inroads by private enterprise into the social service sector are part of a definite trend, much of it imported from the United States, of having private corporations organize large-scale services in child care, hospitals, nursing homes, children's group homes, long-term care, and other areas. These private chains may charge their customers directly or receive a flat rate from the government – getting, for example, so many dollars per bed. Private companies promising to deliver services at lower cost are music to the ears of fiscally challenged governments. Furthermore, once these for-profit social services win government contracts, they have strong incentives to cut their costs further.

In a review of the available evidence about privatization, Canadian economist Ernie Lightman (2003) focused on Accenture, a U.S.-based multinational corporation that offers "global management consulting, technology services, and outsourcing." Lightman studied the company's experiences in working within a number of different countries to help them cut welfare caseloads and costs and found: "In none of these cases did the expected cost savings and efficiencies emerge." The state of Nebraska was one of the places that bought into Accenture's services. The state auditor remarked: "I've been auditor for six years now and this is the most wasteful project I have ever heard of. It's like pouring money down a deep dark hole" (Lightman 2003: 108). From his review of numerous other examples, Lightman concluded: "The evidence overwhelmingly suggests that quality is rarely maintained and promised cost savings are often elusive or non-existent. The case for commercial delivery [of social services], it appears, may have to rest on ideology, an approach for which no evidence is either required or desired" (109).

Business management approaches invariably involve a detailed specification of service inputs and outputs, with each part measured and costed out. What this trend means for social services, as researchers Lena Dominelli and Ankie Hoogvelt point out (1996: 45–62), is that caring for others becomes a commodity to be bought and sold as part of a business transaction. In these exchanges social services are increasingly quantified and price-tagged in competitive bidding for contracted-out services. Dominelli and Hoogvelt note that such contracted-out projects often result in lower rates of pay for service providers. Moreover, they indicate that this business approach, which began a number of years ago, is part of a worldwide restructuring led by global corporations aimed, in part, at lowering labour costs.

Is it surprising, then, that social work services, in seeking to minimize costs, come to embrace the corporate model – which ultimately leads to the abandonment of service users who cannot afford the market price? This trend is obvious in the steady growth of private social work practice, sometimes called "independent" practice. Ironically, one reason for the growth of private practice has been the disenchantment by professionals at the social control over their practice by social service managers. As a result some social workers have decided to manage their own social services by setting up private offices, much like dentists or lawyers, and charging fees for their services. Sometimes several social workers have joined together in partnerships or other arrangements, or have formed consulting firms seeking contracts – for example, to carry out staff development programs for established social agencies.

Social workers who have opted for private practice do succeed in escaping the regulations and policies of social agencies. Yet, although these social workers are no longer constrained by bureaucratic rules, they create a different kind of constraint by bringing the principles – and necessities – of capitalism directly into their delivery of services.

To generate profits these workers must charge a fee for their service. Who will be able to pay? Usually, it is a middle-class clientele. In exchange for payment, such clients receive counselling on how better to cope with psychological tensions, work pressures, and personal troubles.

Private practitioners also obtain funding from government agencies that, for example, contract out family assessments to be used in juvenile court. When social workers carry out such contracts for a state agency, they come back full circle in collaborating with the state. True, they have won a measure of independence in their day-to-day work; they are no longer civil servants. But when they receive government contracts, they are expected to carry out work that does not question the limits on the extent or type of service allowed under these contracts.

Given that the push by business interests for contracting out and privatization have been combined with ongoing lobbying campaigns against unions, it is no surprise that the percentage of workers in labour unions has dropped. At the same time Canadian legislation has removed collective bargaining from many sectors. The Canadian rate of unionization was 27 per cent in 1997. By 2007 it had declined to 25 per cent (Human Skills Development Canada 2008). Indeed, the overwhelming majority of workers in Canada remain outside of collective bargaining.

Roy Adams, a specialist in human rights, notes that the Supreme Court of Canada, in a 2007 case involving B.C. Health Services, affirmed that collective bargaining by workers is a human right. He concludes that we cannot have real democracy when a huge majority of working citizens do not "have the right to negotiate their pay and working conditions with their employers." On the contrary, he says, "They are effectively serfs of unaccountable industrial barons in workplaces that blatantly defile the basic principles of equality, dignity, respect, freedom, and democracy" (2009: 45). Real democracy must include an expanded membership base of organized labour, which is why as progressive social workers we need to intensify our support for labour organizations by pushing for more inclusion of who has the right to full collective bargaining. Without a larger, stronger unionized workforce, business leaders will continue to further escalate privatization and contracting out.

ALTERNATIVE SOCIAL SERVICES

Faced with multiple categories of oppressive social relations, service providers have turned to labour unions as one form of resistance inside social agencies. A different form of resistance, outside of established service structures, consists of developing alternative delivery systems aimed at instituting new, non-oppressive forms of social relations.

For Indigenous people, alternative services mean an alternative to mainstream social services that are often still enmeshed in colonial practices. As part of the political mobilization by First Nations, Métis, and Inuit peoples for self-government, the transfer of social services to Indigenous communities across the country is underway. Aside from being grossly underfunded, these services face an additional challenge: the implementation of services that genuinely reflect Indigenous cultural traditions and aspirations rather than merely reproducing Anglo-centric and Franco-centric social service hierarchies run by Indigenous people.

Despite these barriers, Kathy Absolon is able to write about "surviving and thriving in the landscape of practice." She points to the emergence of a sense of solidarity and nation-building among Indigenous peoples, despite the "government's attempts to divide and pit Indigenous people against one another."

> We have survived the militant attacks and numerous attempts to create divisions in our nations, communities, families, lives and ourselves. Yes, there are many casualties, but today we are still here surviving and in some cases thriving. We talk to one another and show care. We

have the power to dialogue. The voices that we have and the distinct way that we have of telling our story provide us with doorways to free our minds, hearts, spirits and bodies from colonial shackles. Singing, story-telling, dancing, smudging, chanting and talking with one another are healing practices resonating with the sound of our voices and use of our bodies. (2009: 194–95)

Indigenous approaches to building upon cultural traditions are not restricted to a particular agency in a specific region, but rather reflect the construction of alternatives to the continuing, pervasive, colonial domination that exists in Canada. When alternative social services are based on Indigenous knowledge they become important supports to the movement towards self-determination by Indigenous people.

Programs that are alternatives to disrespectful or disempowering social services usually spring from the work of a specific oppressed community or movement: First Nations people, labour union organizations, women, people with (dis)Abilities, racialized and ethnic communities, queer people, local tenants' groups – with women being worse off in each of these groups, which is why women are the majority users of social services. Alternative services emphasize the principle of control by service users over professional services. Examples of alternative social services within the mainstream include establishing a shelter for battered women, a crisis phone line, or a drop-in and information centre.

The women's liberation movement has been especially influential in developing less hierarchical approaches to organizing and delivering feminist services. Many of the newer services are organized as co-ops or collectives so that staff co-operatively make major decisions, often with considerable input from the users of the service. Front-line staff and sometimes users – not only management – have a major say in hiring. The services are often staffed and co-ordinated by people rooted in the particular community being served, people who are personally committed to the reduction or elimination of structural inequalities. Despite the inevitable differences and diversity, they tend to have a shared analysis of the basic causes of problems and what creates the need for their services. As Helen Levine pointed out to me:

"It was no accident that consciousness-raising in small groups sparked the widespread beginnings of the contemporary women's movement. It offered safe space for women to tell the real 'stories' of our lives, to listen to one another without judgment and blame, to grasp the commonalities among us. It was a woman-centred base, grounded in internal and external realities that led to opening up, sharing, analysis and action. I see this as a continuous and essential base in any social change movement."

In another area of social work, Jennifer Ann Pritchard, a graduate of Ryerson's School of Social Work, contrasts her eight years of experience working in bureaucratic group homes with her student experience of working for an organization run by people with (dis)Abilities:

"Group homes give services which are highly individualized, so people with disabilities are kept separate from each other – there's no such thing as meetings, just among people with disabilities. But in self-help groups there's more of a collective sense of potential, hope, possibility, and risk-taking . . . and I found that people with disabilities had a type of camaraderie and humour with each other that's rare in group homes. In the group-home system there's a tendency to deny the disability, to render the person with disability as much like a non-disabled person as possible. By contrast, in self-help groups people embrace their disability, saying, 'This is who I am, dammit. I am as valuable as anyone.' There's a strong sense of validating each other's experience with disability. In this way, people with disabilities are turning the tables on the conventional perception of disabilities as being ugly, not valuable, and a lesser form of life."

Negative attitudes and practices in social services have also had implications for people with diverse experience related to sexual orientation and gender identity. Heterosexism and related negative attitudes and practices among social service providers have resulted in a reluctance on the part of many gay, lesbian, bisexual, and transgendered people to ask for help, as Sarah Todd points out (2006: 384): "As a result, LGBTQ communities are developing queer-positive social services. These organizations are involved in policy change, community organizing, and individual advocacy and service provision." One example of a queer-positive service, in the Maritimes, is the Youth Project. The mission of this non-profit organization is to "make Nova Scotia a safer, healthier, and happier place for lesbians, gay, bisexual, and transgendered youth through support, education, resource expansion and community development." At least two characteristics point to its "alternative" components. First, in its service delivery, "The staff and volunteers present and embody an alternative vision: a place where experiences of hatred and domination are absent, and support education and social opportunities are offered" (Brown, Richard, and Wichman 2010: 163). Second, the organization's decision-making provides a strong voice to youth.

> The Youth Board represents a structural level of governance that institutionalizes the commitment to an inverted hierarchy, where young people are responsible for and resourceful in contributing to the design and implementation of services to meet their needs. Youth Board membership requires that all participants are under the age of 26 years and represent the diversity of experiences and identities surrounding sexual orientation and gender identity. (162)

Another youth-focused organization, Grassroots Youth Collaborative (GYC), specifically calls for a high percentage of its staff and volunteers to be youth:

> The agency should primarily serve youth and be youth-driven, meaning that youth between ages of 13 and 29 years should be fully represented in all areas of the agency and account for over 50 percent of all their volunteers and staff. Youth should also be significantly represented within the board of directors. (Wright et al. 2010: 176)

Other conditions were that the agency had to be not-for-profit and committed to anti-oppression and anti-racism.

Family Resource Programs are yet another area of non-hierarchical and participatory services operating across Canada. The programs, depending on their geographical location and history, are known by a variety of different names: Family Place, Maison de la famille, Neighbourhood House, and Parent/Parent-Child Resource Centre (Child Care Information Hamilton 2009: 1). The staff of these programs provide child care with parent participation and facilitate parent groups that focus on various topics about parenting and related community issues. The programs usually have advisory boards consisting of the participating parents, who help to develop programs responsive to participants' needs. These programs are non-profit and voluntary. A national study found that service users experienced these Family Resource Programs as offering caring and helpful support. One parent who brought her daughter to a program mentioned: "Everyone is so friendly and they made me feel welcome as soon as we walked in the door. Now we come here every day that they are open, and we have been coming here just over a year now" (Silver, Berman, and Wilson 2005: 11). Other parents also praise the program: "It is a wonderful centre that cares about me and my child" (Canadian Association of Family Resource Programs 2009: 17); and "My kids no longer drive me up the wall thanks to the program" (20).

These kinds of alternatives, often supported by progressive social movements and based on the authentic needs of service users and their respective communities, constitute a form of resistance to the mainstream ideologies, narratives, and practices that are often oppressive and are reinforced by conventional agency structures. Social movements offer a different view of personal problems. They see unequal power relations and unequal material resources as major sources of a particular problem or set of problems. Social movements frequently point to visionary ways of reorganizing society based on principles of equity and democratic accountability. For example, some people in the labour movement are now supporting a redesign of the workplace that challenges the typically obscene gap in levels of compensation between executives compared to other employees (Davidson 2010). Still, as Bob Mullaly cautions:

> Anti-oppressive social workers must be careful not to romanticize alternative organizations. Anyone who has ever been associated with such an organization knows how difficult it is to work collectively and cooperatively and to share all decision-making when we, in the West, have been socialized into working and living in social institutions where hierarchy, specialization, and an over-reliance on rules prevail. (2010: 261)

When alternative services become viable, grow, and gain credibility, they can face a new challenge. They want to hire more staff, possibly including social workers, but that requires money. So they draw up proposals and submit them to various branches of government or to a funding agency such as the United Way, asking for funding and taking the risk of co-optation. When governments find that they can't control the alternative services, funds are eventually cut or eliminated. For example, when funds are taken away from some women's shelters and counselling centres, the users either go without support or have to resort to the more restricted sources of aid such as the Salvation Army and welfare departments.

Consequently, alternative services frequently experience uncertainty. Nevertheless, they also represent a hopeful potential. They invite a questioning of top-down structures, and point to a better model of how social programs could be delivered. But changes to democratize social services, while necessary, are not enough to improve service delivery. Generous funding is also necessary.

Furthermore, it is also very important for the voices of service users to truly be heard and respected at the decision-making levels of social agencies; and the voices of service providers and their labour unions are equally indispensable. Better, more effective services are far more likely when staff, front-line workers, supervisors, managers, and funders participate in continuous staff development programs that focus on countering systemic barriers that stand in the way of effective help. Indeed, if such service innovations were in place the need for alternative social services would be greatly reduced.

Meanwhile, in mainstream social service agencies, administrators who feel threatened by such innovations will continue to apply corporate top-down management models, hoping to be rewarded by promotion up the hierarchy. To further ingratiate themselves with their higher-ups, many service managers will act ruthlessly to keep staff and budgets in line and service users in their place. If social work supervisors were able to convince front-line professionals that the best way of helping service users is to accept the agency's constraints, the next step would be for front-line workers to pass this message on to service users. From the vantage point of many service users, that future is already here.

7 REALITY CHECK: SERVICE USERS SPEAK OUT

> The way they look at the dollars – it's like they just ring up their figures on a cash register. You're worth so much for this, so much for that – they make you feel like an animal.
>
> — a woman on social assistance in British Columbia

"Why are we not heard?" It is a question often asked by people who experience oppression. Social services that provide assistance to disadvantaged populations are typically focused on their mandates, their rules, their sense of what is best for others. Jean Swanson, who knows first-hand about being poor and on social assistance, offers this advice in her book *Poor-Bashing* (2001: 188): "People who aren't poor will need to do a lot of listening, be willing to learn, leave space for others, and actively work to end poverty. If we can do this with respect, it could bring together a lot of people who have been separated in the larger struggle for worldwide justice."

If we do a lot of listening, and are willing to learn, we may recognize another person's pain and hear their implicit call for justice. A former welfare client who is a single mother describes her struggle to stay off social assistance.

"By November of last year I went off welfare. I was holding down two jobs, one with the Y, the other with a day care, but the salaries were terribly low. I was bringing in $100 less than when I was on welfare. So I got a third job, at another day care. All these jobs were for different times of the day, different days of the week, but it ended up I was work-

123

ing from 8:30 a.m. till 6 p.m. for five days a week, juggling these three jobs. It was hard but I just never wanted to go back to welfare. I felt I was better than dirt."

Why does receiving assistance make someone feel like dirt? People internalize the stigma against welfare for many reasons. One woman on social assistance said that it wasn't much different from her experience of being married – either way you get *"put down all the time – that's pretty hard for the head to take!"* She adds:

"My rent just went up $125. Welfare tells me to find somewhere cheaper. I tell them I've been looking and even got a letter from the housing registry that says I should stay where I am because I'm paying the going rate and there are so few vacancies in Vancouver. But welfare won't pay for the increase . . . you get to feel that they're blaming me for the fact my husband took off."

Another welfare client put it this way: *"As a single parent on welfare, you feel so vulnerable, so unprotected. You're game for the weirdos on the streets. I've got a double lock on my door, but that doesn't stop the strain – the strain is financial and emotional and it can get to your health too."*

Service users are reminded again and again, sometimes subtly and sometimes not so subtly, that they come from a class, gender, or racialized group, or have a sexual orientation, (dis)Ability, or other identity, that is deemed inferior.

For women, being on social assistance can lead to other problems. *"I did a favour to this neighbour, she was going into hospital to have a baby, so I offered to babysit her two children. Fine? Her husband comes to my place and you know what he wants? He wants to go to bed with me! I refuse and he says, 'You'll be sorry.' He figures I'm on welfare, I'm a single parent – I'm fair game. I told him where to go."*

That kind of treatment month after month demoralizes service users. Given that the amount that social assistance departments allow for rent is typically much lower than the actual rent charged, recipients end up having to make up the difference from their food budgets. In Canada about 1,400,000 people are on social assistance (Human Resources and Social Development Canada 2006). In some provinces people on welfare are allowed to receive financial supplements to buy food, but these are only in the form of a loan. As one person on social assistance said: *"They'll subtract this amount from your next cheque, so you're short next month and you always end up being short. Always behind. You get the feeling that's the way they want it."*

The dynamics lead to clients feeling trapped. Even when, as happens occasionally, the rates are raised, the trap remains. *"Sometimes welfare gives us a raise – at last. We won't be eating macaroni. But nothing changes. Because then the rent goes up and wipes out the raise."* The irony here is that this woman was living in public housing: the rent was raised by the public housing authority. What one branch of government was "giving" with one hand, another branch was taking away with another.

Continual demoralization often leads to further personal crises, shattering the welfare recipient's sense of self – what remains is a shadow of the person, which is then duly imprinted by service providers onto the official files of the state: *"Of course you never see the files that welfare keeps on you. If you're in the office and the worker gets called out, she'll take your file with her. Yet it's our life! So they have us by the strings. We're their puppets. And you better dance!"*

The gulf between social service user and worker is often oppressive. One woman who was on social assistance arranged with the welfare office to get a homemaker who would come into the household and help with child care and other domestic chores.

"Once I got called to the welfare office – this was after I'd had a homemaker. Welfare wanted to know – how come I didn't have enough sheets on the bed? How come there weren't enough clothes? When I came home with a few friends, I could tell the homemaker thought we were all going to be drinking. It so happens I don't drink! But they still wanted me to explain. They even asked me, how come I didn't have any coffee or tea? I was furious. I told them I go without what I like so my kids can have what they need, but I guess they couldn't understand that. Before I could even have this homemaker, they wanted to know where I was going, what I was going to do, everything."

Once again, a sense of fear permeates social assistance. A service user in the Maritimes said: *"When I applied for welfare, I even knew the amount I was entitled to. It was higher than what my social worker said – but I was afraid to push for it. I was reluctant because of fear – I might lose all of it. I can now see how you become too dependent on the worker – how women's passive roles are reinforced by welfare."*

How can these and so many other examples of mistreatment happen in Canada, a country with a Charter of Rights and a reputation for being a good place to live? Service users, social workers, social critics, and government officials have known for years that all was not well with social services.

WELFARE "REFORM": SMOKE AND MIRRORS

Some four decades ago the Special Senate Committee on Poverty (1971: 83) provided the public with a glimpse into what it saw as a highly unsatisfactory situation. It commented critically on the approach then used by social assistance offices: "It repels both the people who depend on the hand-outs and those who administer them. Alienation on the part of social assistance recipients and disenchantment on the part of social assistance administrators were evident in much of the testimony."

In 1997 Senator Erminie Joy Cohen presented her report *Sounding the Alarm: Poverty in Canada*, in which she concluded: "The government of Canada has made many promises to the international community to protect the lives and livelihoods of its most vulnerable citizens. Yet to date, it has made no progress in this area" (1997: 44).

As a result, users of social services frequently face a dehumanizing experience in which human need is given short shrift – a situation confirmed by the persistence of poverty and growing inequality in Canada (Scott 2009: 1). Even before the most recent round of cuts to social programs, the National Council of Welfare, an organization that gives voice to low-income people, stated, "Welfare rates across Canada are so low they can only be described as punitive and cruel." The Council found that in the previous year, "with few exceptions," the incomes of people living on social assistance had deteriorated due to "cuts, freezes and the eroding cost of inflation. Welfare incomes were far below the poverty line in all provinces and territories" (2004; see also National Council of Welfare 2008).

Despite such reports going back for many years – all a matter of public record – little or no progress has been made to end poverty. By the latest count, over three million Canadians live in poverty (Yalnizyan and Klein 2009: 1). Furthermore, about 300,000 people across the country experience homelessness every year (Shapcott 2009: 221). In 1989 the Canadian House of Commons unanimously passed a resolution stating, "This House . . . seeks to achieve the goal of eliminating poverty among Canadian children by the year 2000." Campaign 2000, a national anti-poverty organization carrying out public education, notes that in 2009 "760,000 children and their families in Canada – almost 1 child out of every 9" were still living in poverty. That figure does not include First Nations communities, where one in every four children was growing up in poverty (Rothman 2009).

Marjorie Griffin Cohen, professor of political science and women's studies at Simon Fraser University, Vancouver, reviewed social assistance policies in British Columbia and concluded:

> The process of seeking income assistance has become so restrictive, and so complicated to navigate, that it is systematically excluding from assistance many of the very people most in need of help. The result is a very rapid spike in homelessness and increased hardship in B.C. Our long-term study with people on social assistance indicated that a large number were denied assistance. To survive, they returned to abusive relationships, or relied on panhandling, illegal activities, or the sex trade. Some are living on virtually no income on the streets. (2009: 22)

All social programs are under fire in Canada. At issue is whether our nation's wealth will be distributed according to principles of fairness and equity, or will a relatively small group of people with their gigantic amount of illegitimate privileges block progress towards social justice? The erosion of social programs ranging from medicare to old age security leads to less and less fairness and equity across the country. Social services have become less and less effective.

Funding cuts have been so deep that often services have become impersonal, rushed, and uncaring. Child protection agencies are supposed to help families protect children from harm. Based on interviews with 125 parents, researchers Gary Dumbrill and Winnie Lo, both former social service providers in child protection agencies, concluded that parents who received services from child protection agencies were facing a lack of respect. More specifically, parents believed they were harmed by the social services. They felt judged and misrepresented. It seemed to them that power had been used arbitrarily over them (2009: 133). One mother said that child protection workers "sit there to degrade you and you try to get ahead and to be a better person and they belittle you and it's wrong" (133). Another parent said: "I'd agreed [to my child going into care] for a weekend and that weekend turned out to be six months" (134; see also Strega 2009).

Meanwhile, instead of recognizing the harm to social programs due to tax cuts, Ottawa rejected the recommendation by the United Nations Human Rights Council that the federal government develop a national strategy to eliminate poverty. The federal government asserted that under the Canadian Constitution the provinces and territories have jurisdiction over social policy. But as the public interest organization Canada Without Poverty points out (2009: 1,2): "The federal government has historically played a critical direct or indirect role in influencing poverty outcomes, for example through the introduction of federal income support systems for children in low-income families and for seniors. Moreover, the federal government's response is an affront to the calls to date from several provinces for federal-provincial partnerships to combat poverty."

Canada's failure to address poverty effectively contrasts with the challenge of the United Nations' International Covenant on Economic, Social and Cultural Rights, which calls upon participating states "to recognize the right to social security . . . and to recognize the right of everyone to an adequate standard of living, including adequate food, clothing and housing" (Office of the United Nations High Commissioner for Human Rights 2009). Canada signed this covenant in 1966 and ratified it in 1976; yet by 2004, according to a detailed assessment, the government had taken "little action" to carry out its provisions (Riches 2004: 32).

Similarly, the Assembly of First Nations gave the federal government a failing grade for not implementing the major recommendations made by the 1996 Royal Commission on Aboriginal Peoples. A decade later the federal government had provided "no sustained investment in meeting the basic needs of First Nations communities, or in addressing key determinants of health/well-being" (Assembly of First Nations 2005: 2).

The task of tackling racism shows similar policy failures. A comprehensive report by the National Anti-Racism Council of Canada found an extreme violation of the economic, social, and cultural rights of racialized citizens and immigrants living in Canada (2007: 7–8). Of course, no politician would openly say, "I don't care about racism. I don't care about social programs." Therefore, to sugarcoat their gradual abandonment of social programs, most politicians and business leaders have become adept at spouting soothing, bland words that hide their destructive intentions. Larry Elliott, a writer for the *Guardian Weekly*, decodes their actual meaning, which he supplies in brackets:

> We must become more flexible [accept lower pay] and dynamic [enjoy fewer work benefits]. Rigidities [trade unions and social programs] must be eliminated so that we can be more competitive [companies can make bigger profits and pay less tax] when facing the new global challenge. [If you don't like it, Buster, there are plenty of people in low-wage countries willing to take your job.] (2004: 17)

Among the consequences of these policies failures are more people left behind as jobless and poor; and children who live with the daily experience of their family's hardship. The Child Poverty Action Network (2009) provides a sampling of what children say about their experiences of poverty:

"Feeling ashamed 'cause my dad can't get a job."

"Hiding your feet so the teacher won't get cross when you don't have boots."

"Sometimes it's hard because my mom gets scared and she cries."

"Being teased for the way you are dressed."

At the same time unemployment in Canada is worsening. Over 400,000 full-time jobs were lost between October 2008 and April

2009 (Campbell 2009: 32). This sharp decline was largely due to the spillover of the October 2008 financial crash in the United States, which was caused by financial institutions engaging in speculative and unethical practices that could no longer be sustained (30–31). Yet even before this steep economic downturn, the rules for who can qualify for employment insurance were constantly changing to screen out more and more applicants. Armine Yalnizyan and Seth Klein report (2009: 1): "In 1991, the middle of the last recession, 78% of Canada's jobless received Employment Insurance (EI) benefits. By 2008, that number had fallen to 39% – and only 36% of unemployed women received EI." Although it is supposed to protect the casualties of an ailing economy, the Canadian social safety net is being shredded and is unable to provide effective help to most people who become unemployed through no fault of their own.

With limited access to decent jobs, crime can appeal as a career, which in turn closes more doors. A young Black Maritimer gave a graphic account of the impact of racism and a "clouded" personal history when a job referral agency sent him out for an interview:

"So I called and made an appointment. When I went up to the office, there were two women sitting in the waiting room. I sat down and waited too. This fella comes out of the office and calls out my name. I said 'Yes, I'm here' and I stand up. The fella looks up from his file, sees my face and freezes. Why he practically pushed me down on the chair! I knew I had no chance at a job there. And anyhow, whenever I apply for a job right on the application form there's a section that says, do you have a criminal record? When you put down 'yes,' that finishes your chance for a job."

High unemployment not only hurts the most vulnerable in the workforce – women, people of colour, and youth – but also undermines the labour movement's victories from an earlier era, victories that promised a secure income to anyone willing to become employed. When employment insurance benefits run out, or if an applicant does not qualify, the source of support shifts away from the federal government to provincial and municipal social assistance (or welfare) programs.

The Canada Assistance Plan had blocked workfare, but in

response to the business leaders' campaign to urge the federal government to cut social programs, Ottawa repealed the Canada Assistance Plan in 1995. With its repeal, the very minimal national standards that had existed for social assistance were eliminated,
including the right of social assistance applicants to appeal to an
independent tribunal if they were refused assistance. At the same
time as it dismantled such standards, the federal government
shifted to a system of giving provinces block grants for health care,
post-secondary education, and social assistance. This new arrangement, called the Canada Health and Social Transfer (CHST), gave
provinces more autonomy when it comes to how to spend the federal dollars, which opened the door for further reductions in social
service funding.

A number of provinces (including Alberta, Ontario, and British
Columbia) have adopted the most punitive version of workfare – that
is, cutting people off social assistance if they do not accept the specific jobs assigned to them. Variations of workfare exist in most parts
of the country, which means that social assistance recipients (including single mothers with young children) are being compelled to take
job-training and other employment-related activities; non-compli-
ance results in reduced assistance. Coercion is the common element
in the various workfare schemes. It is based on the prejudice that the
poor are lazy and a big stick is necessary to get them to work.

The contested terrain of social services now includes conflicting
views about whether workfare is a success or failure. Leaders in business and government usually sing the praises of workfare because it
is often followed by a drop in the number of people on social assistance and therefore a further reduction in government spending on
social services. Workfare boosters also claim that the program defeats
poverty because people formerly on social assistance have presumably found jobs. Linda Snyder of the University of Waterloo reviewed
both the U.S. and Canadian experiences with workfare and came up
with a more sober and realistic appraisal:

> Although much of the political rhetoric attempts to suggest that work-
> fare gives "a hand up" to social assistance recipients, empirical evi-
> dence reveals that, while social assistance caseloads have decreased,

the economic well-being of many former recipients has worsened. Many people are no longer eligible for social assistance and have found employment in the precarious low-paying, part-time, and temporary job market. Their earnings and benefits, minus their employment-related expenses for such costs as child care and transportation, frequently provide less than what they were receiving earlier in welfare benefits. The social consequences of this poverty are borne disproportionately by groups already experiencing oppression due to gender, race and class. Women are particularly disadvantaged in the provisions that require them to work, but that do not recognize the realities or the importance of their child care responsibilities. (2006: 325)

While the poor are punished, workfare rewards the rich. Forcing people off social assistance results in specific "savings" for government budgets in social services, which fits well with the tax cuts demanded by people in the most privileged and affluent strata of Canadian society. In addition, when workfare provides a pool of workers for the precarious low-wage sectors of our economy, business corporations benefit from the ability to keep wages low. When political and business leaders team up, as they have done historically, to further undermine labour unions through legislation or repression, labour costs are pushed down even more, creating further benefits for employers, who can smugly smile all the way to the bank.

DIVERSE SOCIAL SERVICES, DIVERSE REALITIES

Today large numbers of Aboriginal children remain in the child welfare system – even more than at the height of the residential schools (First Nations Child and Family Caring Society of Canada 2010: 1).

Elana Beaver, a young Cree woman, grew up in Alberta, where she spent all of her childhood in the care of the province. She recalls her experience:

In Aboriginal history, many youths, generation after generation, were never told about Native residential schools . . . and a lot of the troubles that Aboriginal people had to go through in North America. As for myself, I'm a survivor of the youth protection system. Not knowing about my culture, and my traditions, and my ancestry – was hard to deal with as I was growing up. Many children that grow up without knowing who they are – tend to be lost – and do not have respect for their elders, for themselves or people around them. (2004: CD 4)

From any young child's point of view, separation from parents can be a frightening and bewildering experience. While social work professionals have an adult view of how it all fits together, children usually experience powerlessness and confusion. Social workers, emergency shelters, courts, police, foster parents, group homes, and other institutions: they form a maze that adds to the anxiety. One child compared his experience to being a ball in a pinball machine, with the buttons being pushed by the social services system and the child bouncing from one hard place to another.

This "bouncing" is quite disconcerting when traumatized children are taken into care, only to be re-victimized. All too often when children come into the care of social services, they are sent to group homes where they do not receive good care – which results in some children acting out in aggressive ways. In response the group facility calls the police or security, and the children end up being criminally charged under the Young Offenders Act. Before they know it they get locked up in detention centres for youth (Finley 2004: CD 4). A young person in Quebec describes this pathway from protection to detention:

> I was a victim of sexual abuse and I was locked in – a prison basically, and I was stuck with all these criminals. I felt I had to measure up to them. I wasn't a criminal at the time – [but being there] made me more aware of criminal activity and I did start doing some pretty bad things. But I wanted to be like my peers – otherwise I would have gotten beaten up, or I would have been the outcast and I didn't want that. I felt like I had to be a criminal in order to survive. (Voices of Youth in Care 2004: CD 4)

Social services ignore the needs of children in many ways. A teenage girl in Alberta expressed confusion about the social worker's conduct: "*After they found out about the incest, after they knew what happened, the social worker came over to the house. And the social worker talked to everyone else. She talked to my father, she talked to my mother, but she never talked to me. I want to know why? – why the social worker didn't take into consideration what the victim feels like? It's like you're the one that did something wrong! You're the bad egg! And meanwhile my father gets to stay in the house and I get sent away!"*

The correctional system, which includes prisons for people convicted of crimes, also provides social services, and a goal of those services is the rehabilitation of the offender. I asked a prisoner about this goal: *"Rehabilitation? I get a laugh when a judge says he's giving you a jail sentence so you can get 'rehabilitated.' What rehabilitation? It's a big farce. There's only rehabilitation in the imagination of the judge. When you get sent to prison, there's a piece of paper and it tells them to take you from point A to point B. Point B is prison. The prison gets the piece of paper and the only thing they do, they try to keep you there."*

For years it has been known that prisons do more than just "try to keep you there." A young girl in the Burnaby Youth Secure Custody Centre said, "So where was my rehabilitation when I watched my friends get the shit kicked out of them by uniformed guards?" (Justice for Girls 2003). Rebecca Aleem, representing a public interest advocacy group, Justice for Girls International, finds that in British Columbia, "When girls are put into prison, they frequently experience violence and unjust treatment" and that as many as 18 per cent of girls in custody have attempted suicide (2009: 13, 9). These practices are likely to be no better for the rest of Canada.

The revolving-door syndrome common within prisons and mental-health services means that more often than not service providers fail in their rehabilitation efforts – and it is the punitive nature of the institutions that prevails: *"You get hardened. So if I'm walking down a cell block and someone is stabbed, I keep walking. I don't see nothin' and I don't say nothin'. You keep your mouth shut for your own good."*

Such accounts from people in prisons and mental hospitals led Bonnie Burstow and Don Weitz to note, "The hospital, alas, turns out to be as much a prison as the prison is a madhouse." In their classic book *Shrink Resistant*, they present vivid accounts by "inmates" of their lives in mental institutions. Burstow and Weitz conclude: "Once locked up ... you are more likely to be abused if you are Black, Native, female, gay, poor or old" (1988: 24, 25).

Older adults often spend the last years of their lives in nursing homes or other institutions. Unless you are rich, institutions for the elderly provide a shock for people who have believed in the myth that our society and its institutions take care to provide for our essential well-being. Protecting the well-being of residents in nursing homes often requires the personal support and advocacy of family members and friends. But such individualized attention is usually not enough to improve conditions. More typically, investigative news reports or other initiatives are necessary to draw public attention to unacceptable conditions within what are now being called "long-term care facilities."

For example, in 2004 Bev McKay of Cochrane organized a public forum calling on the Government of Alberta to "enact an effective inspection and enforcement system to act as a strong deterrent to abuse and neglect" in nursing homes. At the forum she asked for a moment of silence "for those who suffered neglect or abuse or those who have died" in these institutions as a result of abuse or neglect. McKay noted that so far the Alberta government had either been "in deep denial or turning their backs" on these issues (Cygman 2004).

The barriers set up by institutions that are supposed to be helpful are faced by many different client populations. Judy MacDonald and Gaila Friars give one example: "Applying for and receiving disability benefits (including Workers Compensation, Canada Pension Disability, and private disability benefits) can often be a grueling process that leaves the (dis)Abled person feeling pathologized, disbelieved, and outright unworthy" (2010: 149).

At times service users themselves are able to successfully oppose questionable behaviour on the part of social service workers. Welfare regulations allow service providers to inquire whether people on social assistance are receiving extra money from any other sources, which according to social assistance rules must be subtracted from the allowance. This practice allows social assistance officers to pry into the private lives of social assistance recipients in ways that can be humiliating. One service user was still fuming at her experience:

"This friend of mine had no job, had no place to go. I agreed to help him out. I admitted him to my place. He wasn't living with me, he wasn't giving me money. I was just trying to help him out. This causes

welfare to investigate me. Now they tell me I have to report all overnight guests. Then they tell me I had to come to the welfare office. I went with an advocate from a community group. I get down there and this inspector tells us, 'All people on welfare are public property!' Can you believe it!? We're now 'public property'!! I got so mad!! I told him why not put me and my children in a zoo?! Can you believe it? I was lucky I had witnesses who heard him. This just gives you some idea what we have to put up with."

In this instance, the social assistance recipient was part of an anti-poverty organization whose members gave each other moral support and realized when the agency was overstepping even its normally punitive boundaries. But most service users are not so fortunate. More often than not such conduct by the agency would proceed unreported and uncontested because most clients – women especially – are verbally beaten down, socially isolated, and worn out just surviving.

Such heartaches sometimes leach into the feelings of social service providers. One person, a member of a client advocacy group, told me about getting a call from a social worker who didn't even want to give her name: *"She told me how she'd tried and tried to help a client, but she said 'the system wouldn't let me.' She burst out crying over the phone."*

CARING SOCIAL SERVICES: TAKE A DEEP BOW

Although service users frequently experience mistreatment in their contact with social services, not all service users have a negative experience. For example, a young service user speaks about his experience with services from the Canadian Mental Health Association:

> I feel happy and proud because I've overcome my mental illness in some ways. I have learned coping mechanisms that have helped me a lot from my very helpful social workers and myself. These coping mechanisms have helped me stay stable so I haven't been in hospital for two years. My relationship with my father is improved from before. I've worked in different jobs and have kept a job for a year. (Gauci, Bartlett, and Gray 2004: 5)

Similarly, an older adult explained, as she brushed away tears, why she was so happy with the Yellow Door, a Montreal social agency that has served older adults for many years: "The Yellow Door changed my life, I don't feel lonely anymore. . . . I feel like they're my family" (Carniol 2004: A6).

In a study of several community-based social agencies in Toronto, social work educator Purnima George asked service users about their experiences with these agencies. Here is a sample of what they told her:

> "I have gained inner peace. I have become more sure of myself. I have learned to make decisions myself, recognize rights and responsibilities . . ."

> "I wanted to protect my husband even though he had beaten me very badly. In my culture, husband is number 1 . . . and I was going to plead guilty in the court. It is this agency that opened my eyes."

> "Activism . . . It's amazing when you come together as a group on the street. It may not change initially, but we are not alone."

> "Now I feel equal with men. . . . I have my goals in life. I have taken my life in my hands and so the life is different for me now." (George 2004: 10,12)

When I asked Purnima George what she thought about these responses, she replied: "*I was amazed – It was very touching for me. I found that service users felt they were transformed. From having no self-esteem to finding their inner strengths. From being fatalistic to taking charge of their lives. From feeling they could not succeed, to succeeding in developing new skills.*"

When I asked her about the approach used by service providers, she said: "*They used a structural approach to social work. These service providers started with where the person was – they focused on social care, getting basic material resources. Getting those resources represented small victories, and made possible the next step. These workers do have a perspective – one that addresses root causes of problems. Workers encourage questions and reflections about the users' beliefs, for example racist beliefs, or sexist beliefs. The worker is careful not to impose an answer, even though conflicting ideas, opinions and meanings are dis-*

cussed. But the answer is provided by the service user, not imposed by the worker."

Purnima George, Brienne Coleman, and Lisa Barnoff, all part of the School of Social Work at Ryerson University, report on feedback from nineteen service users from three different social agencies in Toronto using structural social work:

> "People that work there actually want to help people . . . they don't just stereotype you. You know they give you a chance."

> "I am not a macho man anymore. I always wanted to be right. Now I think what is best for me and my wife. They help you to control yourself. They help you to control your emotions. For me it has been like going to a school to learn, to change myself."

> "Since I came to this agency I see a hundred percent change in myself. When I came here, I was terrified, was not capable of doing anything. I was thinking that death was my solution. Now, I have my goals in life. . . . It seems like a dream to me for who I am now. Often I ask 'Am I the same person?'" (2007: 10, 16, 17)

These examples of good practice and satisfied service users are just a small sample of the constructive help that is being delivered by social services across Canada (Wa Cheew Wapaguunew Iskew [Peacock] 2009). Yet these instances of good practice are just tiny pockets within a much larger reality: a sea of oppressive experiences that service users must endure in social assistance offices, child protection agencies, correctional institutions, and a host of other social services across the country. Nevertheless, these examples of constructive practice, while exceptions to the norm, do offer hope. They also demonstrate what is possible for all social services to accomplish – if certain changes are made. This brings us to issues of social change and the role of service providers, service users, and their allies in contributing to that change.

8 TOWARDS LIBERATION

Remember this: We be many, and they be few. They need us
more than we need them. Another world is not only possible,
she is on her way. On a quiet day, I can hear her breathing.
— Arundhati Roy, World Social Forum, Porto Alegro, Brazil

In 2001 Arundhati Roy, a social activist writer from India,
reminded us of the countless people, near and far, who are
striving for a world free from the multiple oppressions that are
so destructive to the lives of people on this planet. More recently, and
closer to home, Donna Baines has also emphasized that social workers oriented towards progressive change "are not alone." They have
allies everywhere in the movement for social justice, both locally and
globally – "clients, anti-poverty activists, unions, the women's movement, anti-racist groups, Indigenous organizations and anti-globalization activists." They have professional allies among people in
other occupations, people who face similar conditions: nurses, teachers, and academics, for instance. But that is not all: "Policy analysts,
community development workers, public officials and those working
in progressive think tanks and research institutes also share common
ground in this struggle to shift social priorities and resources to those
at the margins in society" (2007d: 195).

These allies provide a supportive context for social service workers who are striving to seek ways of counteracting the oppressive
conditions, narratives, attitudes, and practices that are so harmful to
the people we work with. What all of us need to reach for, on a daily
basis, is to find ways of challenging these injustices.

CHALLENGING MULTIPLE OPPRESSIONS

Lisa Barnoff writes that as part of our work we must find "a way to make space to work on multiple forms of oppression" while also recognizing "their key differences" (2002: 324). This brings us to the suffix "ism," which provides a short-form way of referring to the multiple oppressions stemming from colonial*ism*, rac*ism*, sex*ism*/patriarchy, capital*ism*, heterosex*ism*, age*ism*, able*ism*, and other types of power over others that have embedded themselves into our lives. In addressing these "isms," and how they differ from each other, we need to also consider how they operate in our own individual lives – including how they influence our attitudes – in our efforts to find ways of providing respectful, effective help to social service users.

If I am an Indigenous person, how does colonialism affect me? If I am a non-Indigenous person, do I recognize my illegitimate colonial privileges? What impact does sexism/patriarchy have on my gender reference? Do I experience benefits or disadvantages in relation to patriarchal attitudes and practices? What is my socio-economic class? What kinds of restrictions and/or benefits do I experience due to my class location? Do I experience stigma or receive privilege based on my sexual orientation? How does ageism have an impact on me? Do I have a physical or mental (dis)Ability, or not, and how does ableism affect me? Do I experience privilege or disempowerment because of racism? Do other systemic structures of oppression and privilege have an effect on my life, and in what ways?

These questions address the multiple identities that each of us has. Our answers give us information about our *social location* – that is, about our individual, lived experiences with reference to all these diverse areas of differential power (Carniol 2005b).

Still, as we reflect on the identities that make up our social location, we need to avoid classifying ourselves or others into stereotypes. For example: all women are this; all men are that. In contrast to those kinds of generalizations, we need to understand that other people who share our identity possess a variety of differences in behaviour, attitudes, and expectations. Additional dimensions of difference – for example, among women – may be due to a different cultural background, or different class position, shades of skin colour, sexual orientations, ethnicities, ages, physical or mental abilities/(dis)Abilities, or other differences due to dynamics of privilege and oppression. These systemic differences also have an impact on men given that men continue to be privileged by receiving sexist benefits due to patriarchy. So too, systemic differences have their own impact on other people of privilege just as they do on people who experience disempowerment from each of the "isms."

At times these different identities within our social location will create personal tensions because we become pulled in opposite directions. Sometimes our identities will provide us with privilege, and sometimes they may create disadvantages. For example, an African-Canadian woman may experience vulnerabilities due to her gender and skin colour, yet she also gains a certain privilege from being non-Indigenous. Akua Benjamin, a Black social work educator and activist at Ryerson University, experienced this phenomenon. She recalled one time when she was having a conversation with an Indigenous friend: *"She turned to me and asked, did I realize I was part of the oppression of her people? I was shocked; totally speechless. Me? An oppressor? My ancestors were forced as slaves to come from Africa. We were forced onto ships which brought us to the Americas – to labour in horribly cruel conditions. While First Nations were being exterminated, we were slaves – so how could I be an oppressor?*

"Then I stopped myself and reflected. I listened again to what she had said, but this time I heard her as an ally, as if by a second ear. It was a rude awakening. I'm in Canada now – and benefiting from what the Europeans had done. Now I'm making my life here without any acknowledgement that this was indeed the First Nations' home, not just their land. This is the unsightliness of privilege. We must meet it through a double consciousness. By double I mean for us to develop a critical awareness of our past and present realities of our oppression – and simultaneously of our power and privilege. I should add, as a matter of historical record, many slaves survived as a result of the assistance of First Nations peoples."

The lesson here is that those of us who are non-Indigenous do not escape the benefits of colonialism, even if we experience disadvantage from other parts of our social location. Moreover, even if we dedicate our efforts to building a world free from all oppression, colonial benefits still flow to us because by living in urban or rural environments on land that was stolen from Indigenous people, we are benefiting from the displacement of Canada's first inhabitants.

Does this mean that our personal beliefs, attitudes, and values make no difference? No: they do matter. Our subjective responses to our own social locations and to the locations of others make a critical difference because they are highly relevant to whether we will conform to certain unjust social relations or whether we will oppose them. For example, for me, as a White, middle-class, straight, mainstream male, possessing no serious (dis)Abilities, it does make a difference whether or not I view my privileges as "entitlements." If that is my view, then I will be more likely to consolidate my benefits and privileges. If, on the other hand, I view my multiple privileges as being socially constructed – that is, as structured in ways that funnel benefits to me – benefits that I have not earned – while at the same time causing serious harm to others, it then becomes possible for me to question my privileges and to work for change.

To put it another way, being mindful of my continuously evolving critical consciousness strengthens my capacity to be a social justice activist. As Tracy London puts it, "Engaging in self-reflective emancipatory practice in the fight for justice means there is a unity within one's being as a change agent of oneself and of society" (2009: 199).

Although postmodern perspectives have widened our understanding about the great variations in subjective understandings of people's lived experiences, none of these differences should eclipse an equally important reality: namely, the common social processes that exist among people who experience the same identities and similar social locations. From my experiences with social services and social activism, I became aware of a number of social processes within the divided world of "haves" and "have-nots" pertaining to the privileges attached to both single and multiple identities.

Of course, I am also aware that I am not the only person who has witnessed, for example, that when individuals gain substantial benefits at the expense of others due to their illegitimate privilege, something else happens. These individuals not only tend to see themselves as "superior" to others, but they will also tend to define their privileges as "entitlements." As part of this process, people who are disempowered due to their lack of privilege tend to be viewed as "less than" by the privileged. This tendency in turn has further consequences. The privileged and their supporters will subject disempowered populations to a steady barrage of harmful prejudices, oppressive narratives, and contempt. These combined processes result in a justification of privilege, which becomes "normalized" and therefore invisible to most privileged people as well as to many others.

A further result is that many disempowered individuals will themselves engage in processes that also "normalize" these oppressive narratives. In doing so, individuals who are already disadvantaged further undermine their self-images by internalizing negative stereotypes about themselves into their psyches. This condition in turn can lead to self-harming behaviour, ranging from addictions to suicide. In response mental health services, related therapies, and social services may try to come to the aid of these "troubled" persons, although the attempted help typically ignores the role of illegitimate privileges. In these ways, problems that have structural or systemic roots are converted by professional helpers into personal problems, as if the source of such problems were "deficiencies" originating entirely from inside the heads of these patients, clients, or service users.

Given the layer upon layer of processes that effectively make these systemic injustices invisible, it is remarkable to witness countervailing social processes whereby individuals who are disempowered by one or more identities are sometimes able to shift their attitudes about being mistreated – from acceptance to resistance. While such countervailing processes may be understandably slow, under certain circumstances these shifts in attitudes can accelerate with rapid speed.

These circumstances consist of a host of complex and interactive factors. Examples are the emergence of alternative explanations showing that the mistreatment is wrong, the emergence of progressive leaders among the victims and survivors of the mistreatment, the existence of allies among the more privileged segments of the society, and, sometimes, precipitating events that expose the unfairness or brutality of the mistreatment. When many victims and survivors are able to say, "Enough! No more!" they tend to engage in community, political, or personal processes that coalesce in informal networks and formal groups. At times members of these groups and networks will organize themselves to take concerted action to move another step towards emancipation.

From the far side of the oppression-privilege continuum, individuals who benefit from one or more identity often come to recognize their common interest with other privileged individuals. They tend to be motivated to pursue their own process by creating informal networks and formal groups with membership restricted to their exclusive circles in order to further entrench and maximize their benefits. Using the mass media and deploying their considerable financial and material resources, they spend considerable efforts to shape public opinion to defend and support their privileges. For example, they will repeat over and over their belief that their privileges are accessible to anyone who works hard enough. These processes result in the formation of a multiplicity of organizations, such as the Canadian Council of Chief Executives, whose members use their considerable corporate influence to win laws and policies that have the effect of widening the gap between rich and poor (see chapter 2).

By comparison to the special interest groups of the rich, people who have experienced multiple oppressions engage in their social processes to resist the further polarization of rich and poor. They also often point to alternative directions, such as non-oppressive ways of reaching a sustainable and equitable future. Disadvantaged by less power, fewer resources, and lower prestige, a diversity of disadvantaged people still manage to come together in solidarity with each other, sometimes forming social movements to push for social progress. These movements often consist of numerous community organizations. The local groups seek and sometimes obtain support from progressive people, including workers in health, education, and social service organizations.

SOCIAL WORK PRACTICE THEMES FOR LIBERATION

When social service providers apply a structural-social-justice analysis, what does social work practice look like? Social services that provide help to people in ways that pay attention to social justice usually apply practice frameworks known as "structural social work" or "anti-oppressive," "critical," or "progressive" social work – which are also umbrella terms that cover a wide range of more specific practices ranging from feminist to anti-racist approaches.

In their book *Structural Social Work in Action: Examples from Practice* (2010), Steven Hick, Heather Peters, Tammy Corner, and Tracy London invited numerous social work educators and practitioners to answer an important question. Is it possible to actually practise structural social work, or is it just a theory? They conclude:

> It is happening. It is not just a theoretical proposition; it is not romantic idealism. We are engaged in structural social work practice and the chapters in this book are a testament to the fact that it is working. We are making a difference in the lives of clients and in our lives, and we are making changes in societal structures. (2010: 236–37)

In that book, social worker Vivian Del Valle and I co-authored a chapter (Carniol and Del Valle 2010) that relates how Vivian provided counselling to a woman who had been sexually and emotionally abused. The service user, Carolina (not her real name), had come from Latin America to live in Canada with her family. In Canada her son-in-law worked in construction during the day, and his wife worked at cleaning office buildings at night. Carolina looked after their children. Over a period of several years, while his wife was at work, the husband sexually abused his mother-in-law – repeatedly and violently raping her. He threatened to harm her grandchildren if she ever told anyone. When his wife found out about the abuse, she called the police, who investigated and arrested her husband.

Around that same time, Carolina stopped talking to everyone: her silence went on for months. Her distraught daughter took her to a Spanish-speaking social service agency, where Carolina was given an emergency appointment to meet with Vivian, a Spanish-speaking, Latina Mestiza.* Prior to their first meeting, Vivian received a brief summary of what had happened to Carolina.

As Vivian and I wrote our chapter for the book, we identified a number of practice themes that arose from how the social worker in this case (Vivian) provided help.

- Finding voice
- Finding oppression
- Finding resiliency
- Raising critical consciousness
- Standing up for client rights
- Developing solidarity for emancipation.

When we examined these practice themes, we realized that they were also present in other situations in which we had participated as counsellors. We also realized that the themes are not linear; rather, they overlap and are often present simultaneously in various combinations. We suggest these themes, then, not as a mechanical toolbox, but as flexible guideposts for social service providers who want to deliver progressive social services. We believe too that Vivian's practice in this case contains components that are readily transferable to other practice situations.

Finding voice

In Vivian's first interview with Carolina, a long silence followed after Vivian briefly introduced herself. Carolina had brought along her knitting needles and a ball of wool, and started to knit as soon as she had been shown a seat in Vivian's office. During the silence, Vivian was attentive. Realizing that Carolina had not spoken a word for three months, Vivian used non-verbal empathy to give Carolina as much emotional space as needed. Carolina continued knitting while

---

* Latina refers to women from Latin America. Mestiza refers here to a bi-racialized woman having Indigenous and European ancestors.

she slowly looked around at the Latin American artifacts in Vivian's office.

Meanwhile Vivian's goal was to develop a therapeutic alliance with Carolina, as she did with others in her clinical practice. That approach meant that for this first session Vivian refrained from using the usual direct approach of asking questions about the abuse. Instead, she used non-verbal communication skills to express genuine concern and to provide reassurance that in this counselling session it would be safe for Carolina to find her voice. Taking her time, Carolina made eye contact with Vivian, who continued to "tune in" to Carolina's needs.

Vivian's experience and intuition helped her to assess the right moment to comment about the colour of the wool that Carolina was knitting with. In response, Carolina said a few words about the wool. Vivian then gently asked a question about the wool, to which Carolina replied. This interaction gradually grew into a conversation about knitting.

This respectful, non-threatening approach helped Carolina to engage in a conversation for the first time since her son-in-law's arrest. Based on her own cultural awareness, the social worker was able to "be present" to the client's communication needs. She neither rushed in with agency forms to fill out, nor imposed other agency procedures that interfered with the client's ability to find her voice.

Finding oppression

Once Carolina had broken her silence, it was important for the social worker to go on to build a warm, welcoming atmosphere that would help the service user to gradually tell her own very personal and painful story. Carolina's narratives revealed that she had accepted many of the other hurtful injustices that she had experienced throughout her life. During this early stage of weekly counselling sessions that would continue for eighteen months, Vivian, exercising self-discipline, refrained from intervening with her own progressive perspective on what had happened. In allowing Carolina to tell her story in her own way, the worker learned about how the client gave meaning to her own experiences. This approach also allowed for a deeper development of trust to evolve between the worker and service user. At the same time Vivian was making her own assessment by finding how Carolina's lived experience reflected multiple forms of oppression.

Finding resiliency

As a therapeutic relationship developed between them, Vivian helped Carolina talk about what kept her going despite experiencing the trauma of being repeatedly raped, her disgust of feeling trapped, her worry about her emerging symptoms of illness (weight loss and severe skin infections that continued despite prescribed medication), and her fears of putting her grandchildren in harm's way. Carolina spoke about being emotionally nourished by her loving relationship with her grandchildren, and being somehow spiritually strengthened through her own suffering to protect them. When survivors of oppression and trauma are able to find ways of holding on to their crushed sense of dignity, counsellors can help by recognizing and affirming these vital sources of resiliency.

Raising critical consciousness

Carolina spoke about her granddaughter being bullied by a boy at school, telling Vivian that the event did not matter because girls had no rights. By now, having provided clinical counselling to Carolina for a number of months, Vivian sensed that a solid basis of trust existed between herself and Carolina. Vivian decided the time was right for her to tactfully challenge Carolina's attitudes by doing some critical education about gender equality. Vivian told Carolina an abbreviated story about the women's liberation movement: how women had organized themselves and pushed for changes in attitudes, practices, narratives, policies, and laws. By sharing this history of resistance to oppressive social relations, the counsellor was able to help Carolina expand her awareness. When Vivian asked Carolina if she would sign a consent form that would give the social worker permission to contact the school, Carolina agreed. Vivian met with the principal, and the boy subsequently confessed and wrote an apology to Carolina's granddaughter.

Standing up for client rights

Would Carolina testify in court? It is one thing for service users to find their voice in counselling sessions; it is quite another matter for them to speak their truths at public forums such as public hearings, court trials, or street rallies. Carolina wanted to testify in court, but was stymied by her fears of the perpetrator. In response, the social worker, Vivian, was not neutral: she provided educational, emotional, and material support to assist her client, Carolina, to stand up for herself. In helping Carolina prepare for court, Vivian referred her to orientation sessions delivered in Spanish and sponsored by the court to demystify criminal court proceedings. Carolina asked Vivian to accompany her and her daughter to court.

Developing solidarity for emancipation

In court Carolina testified and endured a tough cross-examination. The judge found the perpetrator guilty and sentenced him to prison. The court's verdict gave Carolina a liberating message of hope about abused women being vindicated. Meanwhile, Vivian had teamed up with a Spanish-speaking group facilitator and obtained management support for their co-facilitation of twelve sessions to a group of Latinas who had experienced abuse. Carolina was invited to join these sessions. The group was highly interactive (role-playing, storytelling) and culturally supportive (in Spanish, cultural foods, with a piñata.) The sessions included critical education on such topics as sexual and emotional abuse, systemic oppression, patriarchy, colonialism, internalized privilege, women's rights, and social justice. As a result, Carolina and other group members formed bonds of solidarity with each other, and benefited from a new network of interpersonal support for their growing critical consciousness.

Bob Mullaly points out the value of such groups:

> There is widespread agreement [among many anti-oppressive and progressive social work writers] that becoming part of a group process with other persons who are similarly oppressed is the most effective way for oppressed persons to (1) develop political awareness, (2) self-define a more authentic identity than the one imposed on them by their oppressors, (3) develop the confidence to "come out" and assert

their more authentic identity, and (4) establish solidarity in order to take action against their oppression. (2010: 228)

As I reflect on the ways in which Carolina was helped, I am struck by how group solidarity emerged from a progressive version of social work that allows women to find their voices, affirm their resilience, develop critical consciousness, and stand up for their rights. In contrast with the more conventional forms of practice that shy away from political analysis, structural social workers are "case critical" in at least two ways: first, they are critical of doing the type of casework and case management that ignores or diminishes equity issues; and, second, they apply critical consciousness to themselves by challenging the dynamics of privilege and oppression that play out in their own lives and the lives of others.

SOCIAL MOVEMENTS AND SOCIAL SERVICES

When many people come together to focus on personal and systemic abuses that have a dire impact on their lives, and when they organize themselves over a period of time to demand social justice, they become a social movement. In Canada a multitude of different people have come together in progressive social movements: Indigenous peoples, organized labour, lesbians, gays, bisexual and transgendered people, older adults, women, people with (dis)Abilities, racialized people, anti-poverty networks, human rights activists, and members of diverse cultures. Each social movement expresses its own meaning for its goals by drawing on its own lived experience to shape its social analysis. For instance, as Indigenous people build their social movements, they are developing anti-colonial approaches (see Kine-wesquao [Richardson] 2009; Assembly of First Nations 2010; Métis National Council 2010; Inuit Tapiriit Kanatami 2010). Michael Anthony Hart (Kaskitémahikan) gives his view of that project:

> Anti-colonialism includes actions such as social and political mobilization to de-legitimate and stop the colonial attacks on Indigenous knowledge and peoples. It seeks to affirm Indigenous knowledge and culture, establish Indigenous control over Indigenous national territories, protect Indigenous lands from environmental destruction and

develop education opportunities that are anti-colonial in their political orientation and firmly rooted in traditions of Indigenous nations. (2009a: 32)

The reasons for and the nature of the demands to be treated with respect, as well as the nature of the social change called for – all of these have their own nuances and meanings for participants.

Each of the social movements experiences an ebb and flow of lesser or greater influence, depending on factors such as leadership, geographic region, forces arrayed against it, and shifts in public opinion. Each of the "isms" has resulted in social movements that push back against the injustices caused by the particular "ism." Often the movements will work separately on their respective concerns. At other times some of the different social movements will join together to press for change. Examples of several movements coming together to produce sizeable public support include campaigns focusing on international peace, environmental protection, and anti-globalization. Sometimes social activists will start new community networks. One such activist, Deena Ladd, as a co-ordinator of Toronto's Workers' Action Centre, told me:

"We're starting a new movement of workers who are not unionized because they work on short-term contracts through temp agencies, often working part-time at very low wages. On a personal level, these workers are often quite depressed because they can't get good jobs, and they're often exhausted from working long hours. We work directly with them, giving personal and political support. We show it's possible to fight back.

"When a worker doesn't get paid, we go to the employer. That happened this month with a restaurant employer. Three of us, including the worker, went at the restaurant's most busy time and tactfully but firmly demanded payment. The employer paid part of what was owing, with a promise for the rest next week. We let him know: if he breaks his promise to us, we'll return to leaflet his restaurant customers. And we'll do it if he breaks his promise. Through our work, we break the isolation experienced by these workers. We also do skill development and leadership training. How to use the media? What's policy? Why do employers have so much power? Are you being used?

We have food at our meetings and have fun along the way. We're building relationships and we're also building a membership base."

In 2009 Ladd, working with social policy advocate Trish Hennessy, reported on the progress of this new movement. It had succeeded in convincing the Ontario government to enact legislation giving new legal protections for temporary agency workers, and to provide a multi-million-dollar budget for hiring new enforcement officers to keep employers in line with the law. Ladd and Hennessy note that these small but important steps were the result of workers empowering themselves due to the approach used by the Workers' Action Centre when workers phone for support and advice:

> We start from the position that we're not the experts – they are – and we invite them to get involved by working with others for long-term change. Our workers' hotline delivers support in six languages and becomes a first step for new workers to become involved in our campaign. Every week, we hold sessions for new members, in which we give an overview of basic rights in Ontario and create a safe space to ask questions, share experiences and break the isolation that non-unionized workers face. Something important happens: a group of people who have never met each other begin talking about realities facing them on the job and what's happening in their lives; they start agreeing that what's happening isn't right and that they have a role in doing something about it. Together. Everything we do follows this basic principle: Nothing about us without us. (Ladd and Hennessy 2009: IN5)

As these movements get stronger and form coalitions and alliances with each other, they often raise the political and personal consciousness of the participants (Swift et al. 2003; Hudema 2004; Rabble 2010; Council of Canadians 2010; Real News Network 2010). Sometimes they take to the streets. More often they work within institutions in which members are employed or have other attachments, creating spaces for new non-oppressive social relations, locally and globally (Smith 2008; Bantjes 2007; Rebick 2009).

These movements sometimes include social agencies that push for wider changes while at the same time providing counselling to service users. For example, SOS (Surpassing Our Survival), a sexual assault agency in the interior of British Columbia, helps women and children who have been sexually abused. Dawn Hemingway, Clarie Johnson, and Brenda Roland tapped into their activism with the women's movement as they documented their experience with this social agency's commitment to "unrelenting public education work linked to collective action" (2010: 80).

The combination of education and action is reflected by letters to the editor that sos sent to newspapers in response to sexist media stories, and in its practice of using art creatively – such as quilting to express not only the trauma of sexual violence but also visions of a respectful world. The agency's community work also included providing leadership in Prince George in organizing Take Back the Night, "an internationally recognized event in which women and children march through the streets to highlight their right to live without fear of violence, harassment and sexual assault" (Hemingway, Johnson, and Roland 2010: 80). sos also joined with First Nations and community organizations across the north to march, dance, and drum on Highway 16, to demand action by politicians and the police concerning women, mostly Aboriginal, who had been murdered or gone missing from this road that runs from Prince Rupert to the Alberta border.

In counselling mothers of sexually abused children, sos relies on research showing that in the vast majority of cases the perpetrator's secretive methods prevent mothers from knowing about it. That is why, in its counselling, the agency works to counter the rampant mother-blaming by professionals, including by child protection workers, doctors, teachers, and police. In addition, this social service agency not only has programs for male youth and adult men who have been sexually mistreated as children or as adults, but also works with other community agencies that help offenders take responsibility for their actions and work for personal change. Hemingway, Johnson, and Roland remind us: "Sexual assault is a gendered crime. The reality is not that men are not victims of sexual violence; it is that they are almost always the perpetrators of sexual violence against both women and men" (2010: 88).

When asked why sos does not focus only on its clinical counselling, Hemingway, Johnson, and Roland point out:

We fully understand the importance of day-to-day work that addresses critical, immediate needs. It must be done. But, ultimately, meeting these immediate needs is not very meaningful if not carried out in the context of fighting for longer-term fundamental changes that will eradicate sexual violence. In practice and of necessity, these potentially contradictory approaches are, in fact, concurrent and complementary undertakings. Our belief, borne out by nearly 25 years of practice, is that you cannot successfully do one without the other. (2010: 90)

That is why it is important for social workers and other helping professionals to align themselves with progressive social movements. Without the pressure from social movements, there would be no progress towards equity. That is because the people who are benefiting from the "isms" will typically use their power and privileges to block change. Social movements are the engines that mobilize nonviolent power from the grassroots outward and upward. Under certain conditions, and with the help of allies inside various institutions, social movements can develop enough public pressure to make change happen.

While Canadians still have a huge distance to travel to achieve a full measure of social justice, nevertheless we have seen modest changes in some areas. As just one example, Marilyn Callahan reminds us of progress made due to the women's liberation movement:

When I began to participate in feminist groups in the 1960s, the world was a very different place for women. There were few women in any of the well-paid professions such as law and medicine; divorcing women had no claim to the matrimonial property; First Nations women lost their status if they married nonstatus men; sexual assault was often blamed on women; and most young women did not expect to have a career and marriage at the same time. Dramatic changes have occurred since then and feminist groups can take credit for many of these, working outside and within policy-making structures. (Callahan 2004: 139)

LIBERATION AND SOCIAL SERVICES

In some parts of the world – particularly in police states and places subject to assassinations, HIV-AIDS pandemics, genocide, and extreme poverty – emancipatory efforts are extremely difficult and dangerous. At the same time, we can learn from the progress achieved through struggles, near and far. Baines emphasizes that we can gain inspiration for our struggles at home by looking to "Third World and Indigenous experiments in participatory democracy, participatory budget and policy making, and new forms of collective social support" for examples. Indeed, she argues, "Some of our best hopes for social justice lie in finding common ground and internationalizing our struggles" – that is, in finding ways of supporting and working in solidarity with the struggles for self-determination, peace, and sustainable development taking place around the world (Baines 2007d: 193).

The contested nature of social services in Canada is a small part of the global drama to transform all unjust structures into processes of equity, ecological sanity, authentic democracy, and respect for the diversity of multiple cultures and communities. Such transformation is being nudged forward by a liberated version of professionalism that is beginning to take shape within social work in Canada and elsewhere.

Being fully liberated as a person is probably not possible within an overall system that remains highly oppressive. But it is still possible to be partly liberated, as a person and as a helper, as we push the boundaries to dismantle all oppressions. Part of that process consists of listening to what service users are saying. For example, two single-parent women who self-identify as Native and who had experienced both good and bad service gave me clear messages about what they wanted from social service providers. *"Don't treat me as a number,"* one of them said. *"Take the time to show interest in my life. Don't tell me what to do, but help me figure out what I should do."*

"Be personal," said the other. *"Share a bit of your life with me, so I know who's working with me. Don't just hide behind your desk.*

"When helpers and people being helped know we're all in this together, there's not that thick line dividing us. Then we know we're

here for each other. That's the kind of service I'm part of now – and it's great! It's changed my life for the better. I'm not shy to speak up anymore. I've found my voice, and now I can help others too."

As we listen to people who know about oppression from first-hand experiences, there is much we can learn about how to deliver social services in respectful, effective ways. A group of queer activists, for example, offered some snippets of advice to social service providers:

Do your own work – examine your own beliefs, attitudes, and knowledge about queer people, issues and communities. . . . Examine how you contribute to the oppression, marginalization, powerlessness and exploitation of queer people. . . . Eliminate heterosexist language from your spoken use. . . . Take the challenge to interrupt homophobic and heterosexist behaviours whenever you see them.

In work with individuals – validate the stories of stigma and victimization and connect them to their historical, structural and political origins; listen to the coping strategies, frustrations, and anger and draw from them to develop potential actions that impact social conditions.

In institutions – take active steps to create your agency as one where queer people and heterosexual allies would like to work and/or come for service; develop non-discriminatory and anti-harassment policies for the explicit protection of queer staff and clients; hire, retain, and validate the contributions of queer people. (Brown, Richard, and Wichman, 2010: 169–70)

These plus similar guidelines for social service work with all of the other distinctly disempowered populations need to be implemented throughout all social services in Canada. More than that, these guidelines for respectful practices towards everyone who experiences systemic oppression need implementation in all institutions, including private, public, and NGO non-profit sectors. That includes all schools, banks, and media and on-line communication industries. Achieving this change would represent a significant change towards social justice.

A small step towards such change is for us to become aware of the sources of negative attitudes that we may be holding against people who have been disempowered by one or more of the "isms." Jean Swanson helps us understand a major source of prejudices against people who live in poverty: "Big corporations have to take a huge responsibility for poor-bashing. *They* own the media . . . that accuse people who use welfare of being fraudulent. . . . *They* want poor-bashing policies like low or no minimum wages, welfare cuts, no government job creation, and trade deals that give corporations more rights" (2001: 186). In a similar way, each social movement has its own analysis of the sources of insults and stigma against its members. In learning about these sources, and about how social movements work for change, we need to figure out how we can best be supportive of their social justice goals.

As we listen and learn about what service users and their social movements see as important, our focus becomes the question: what should be the role of helpers? I raised this question with an old friend, Jim Albert, an Indigenous Elder who has taught social work at universities for almost three decades. He is regularly asked to serve as an Elder at ceremonies, to conduct sweat lodges, fasts, and healing circles.

"We have to respect the autonomy of the persons asking for help as they are the only ones that can heal themselves. It's all about relationships. For our part in a helping relationship, we need to know who we are, to learn to respect ourselves in a fundamental way, and to be able to love ourselves. If we are on our own healing journey then we are better able to share our medicines and our skills with those who have asked for help. We have to be very careful that we don't take over someone else's problem, and [we have to] respect their ability to deal with it themselves.

"While we have to respect the autonomy of the individual we also have to recognize that we live in a world where people's rights are constantly being violated through the various forms of oppression that they experience. We need to walk with them and advocate with them and find ways to expose the oppressions and inequalities that they face. We need to walk with others who are on their healing journeys,

to be good role models, and to be prepared to stand in opposition to oppressive practices and policies in the world around us."

Our activities in carrying out these roles are not restricted to formal job descriptions. Luisa Quarta spent some time as a clinical social worker at an agency that works with people who have developmental disabilities, and she describes her approach to practice in that job:

"For me it's important to understand that 'social work practice' doesn't just mean what happens in the office between myself and a client. Yes, practice definitely includes that relationship, but it also includes my relationship with the agency, plus my relationship with community – from local to global spheres. And more, practice includes my relationship to myself. What I mean is – my willingness to enter into self-reflection, and to share this self-reflection with clients. I believe that when we do this personal sharing, it helps to break down the imbalance, the distance between clients and ourselves."

Quarta's story is about a social service agency that had about one hundred and twenty employees and was structured in what she calls *"a racialized hierarchy."* The workers who did housekeeping and clerical work were predominantly people of colour, and the clinical professional staff were predominantly White. She told me about a time when the agency had a new chief executive officer who set out to cut agency costs – although he also clearly wanted to be seen as being fair about it. According to Quarta, *"He had the management prerogative of laying off people and that's what he did. He gave notice and targeted clerical and housekeeping staff for layoffs."*

Quarta and her co-workers were members of a local of the Ontario Public Service Employees Union (OPSEU); she was president of the local. They saw clearly what was happening: at the same time as the agency management was planning to lay off members of the housekeeping and clerical staff, it was spending large sums of money on technology and consultants. *"We knew there were other ways to save money rather than throwing people out of jobs. We felt the layoffs devalued the importance of housekeeping and clerical staff to accomplishing our work. Without question, it would create hardships – some people to be laid off were single parents, women of colour."*

Under the circumstances the union saw the layoffs as immoral and decided to try to stop them. While management tried to de-personalize the layoffs, offering a rationale that offered no recognition of the people involved, the union insisted that the layoffs involved real people. One of the union's first steps was to invite the people threatened with layoff to come to a union meeting. It encouraged them to step forward, to tell their stories, give voice to their experience. *"This created spaces where professionals could learn, sometimes for the first time, about the details of the work done by these employees. The more that the professionals heard about the planned layoffs, the more that opposition grew to this way of cutting costs."*

Luisa Quarta and her co-workers came up with a plan of attack. At the next agency staff meeting every single one of them showed up wearing a black top as a symbol of protest against the layoffs. The agency managers, she said, *"were utterly shocked that the room was a sea of black. . . . The managers cut the meeting short, and two days later announced there would be no layoffs.*

"When we heard the results, tears came to my eyes. Agency staff had never before experienced the power of a collective voice, and now were saying 'we did it!' It was meaningful for me to be part of an experience where we made a material difference to people's lives. We actually prevented people from losing their jobs. We showed that collective resistance can work and that sometimes we can win."

That collective resistance – and the strategy involved – drew upon community organizing skills similar to those used by social workers and others within the wider community. Such community organizing often happens at a local level, and includes creating or strengthening alternative social services, mobilizing social action, and conducting public education in opposition to unjust policies and inadequate services (Lee and Todd 2007; Brown and Hannis 2008).

Going up against the forces of privilege can be risky. People of privilege feeling threatened will typically retaliate, carefully hiding their own positions of privilege as they belittle or attempt to discredit our efforts. They may honestly believe that they favour social justice as they organize a political backlash to protect their privileges (Klein 2008). Amidst such contradictions, they may portray themselves as victims and complain about being unfairly treated, even silenced. This is not easy terrain, which is why activists always need the support of trustworthy allies along the way – which sometimes means creating our own support groups.

Support groups vary in how they get formed, how often they meet, how they function, and how long they last. A support group I belong to is small, consisting of half a dozen people who practise or teach in the social services. We began as an activist group, tackling issues ranging from racism to professional elitism. Our activities have ranged from lobbying public officials to working with media, from sponsoring public educational events to joining large-scale street demonstrations. We meet once a month, which we've been doing for over twenty years. One of our members, Judy Tsao, who works with homeless people, describes how our group provides support:

"As the group evolved, our get-togethers created a space where we could vent our frustrations and receive encouragement from each other. There's a lot of pressure in our work, yet despite the complexities – I felt understood by other members. I felt we had shared values. As we got to know each other, there was relationship-building among ourselves, which to me is so important. The result was amazing – I found the group provided safety for us to express our concerns. It wasn't at all planned, the group seemed to evolve organically, as a few people moved on and new folks came in. We respect and like each other – we became friends. We'll brainstorm about issues and exchange information about resources. We'll go and support picketing social workers out on strike, but our main focus is to give each other support. Knowing I have that level of support adds to the strength I need to do my job."

There is an ancient folk saying: "Where your fear lies, there lies your power also" (Bishop 2002:100). In her writing, bell hooks offers an insight into our fears:

> Dominator culture has tried to keep us all afraid, to make us choose safety instead of risk, sameness instead of diversity. Moving through that fear, finding out what connects us, revelling in our differences; this is the process that brings us closer, that gives us a world of shared values, of meaningful community. (2003: 197)

I am hopeful about celebrating diversity within shared values because

I have seen religious leaders from diverse faith communities, ranging from Moslem to Christian to Jewish, being able to draw upon their spirituality to reach across difference and to provide impressive inspiration for social justice activism (Hashemi 2009; Nhat Hanh 1991; Cole-Arnal 1998; Rabbis for Human Rights 2010; *Tikkun Magazine* 2010). This is in sharp contrast to other leaders from each of these religions who still insist on preaching hate, superiority, and violence.

In light of such mixed messages, it is tempting to become dispirited. We can become even more discouraged if we make an assessment of the social forces lined up against us. To put it another way, how can we be hopeful of social progress when those responsible for the ecological, social, and military disasters hold so much power? Historian and activist Howard Zinn once explained why he was still opting for hope:

> To be hopeful in bad times is not just foolishly romantic. It is based on the fact that human history is a history not only of cruelty, but also of compassion, sacrifice, courage, kindness. . . . We don't have to engage in grand, heroic actions to participate in the process of change. Small acts, when multiplied by millions of people, can transform the world. (1994: 208)

Paul Agueci, a social activist working in the social services, suggests how hope can lead to strength: "*As a person with a disability, I know the importance of support. At the age of ten, I was in crisis, in a coma for three months. I had a huge struggle, and without support from my family and others – I'd be dead now. I'm an activist because I've learned from that experience – people in the disability community can't do it alone. Our survival depends on that support, and I believe that's true for others too. Whether it's people in feminist groups, unions, mental health organizations, or other community networks – it's through support that people find their communal voice. And we're finding that voice. That's what gives me hope. That's what makes us strong.*"

Anne Bishop identifies another source of hope that motivates her social justice activism:

[It] is a vision of a world I would like to live in, a world based on cooperation, negotiation, and universal respect for the innate value of every creature on earth and the Earth itself. This is a world where no one doubts that to hurt anyone or anything is to hurt yourself and those you love most, a world where everyone works to understand what the effects of everything we do will be on future generations. (2002: 150)

Bishop's values are shared by many others, including progressive social workers and helpers whose concerns move far beyond the delivery of enlightened social services (Baines 2007a; Coates 2003; Lavallée 2008; Lysack, 2010; Mullaly 2010; Hick et al. 2010; Sinclair, Hart, and Bruyere 2009; Strega and Sohki Aski Esquuao 2009; Wehbi 2004). In addition to these life-affirming values, I find that what also inspires me is my intuitive sense that human life is a precious, sacred gift – a gift that is violated by the processes of oppression and privilege that inflict massive abuse on people. Most of us have been bruised by such systemic abuse. One effective way of pushing back is by proceeding on our own healing journey that empowers us to strive for social justice. Why work for social justice? Because striving for social justice means reaching for the well-being of ourselves and of others. As we take action with progressive activists locally and globally, we choose a side, join with others, and we resist. We mobilize to take back power for ourselves.

But that power is different than power-over. It stems from our inner agency – that is, from the strength found inside the deep and wide corridors of our inner lives. Our individual capacity to take risks for social justice is nourished by our inner power – our ability to pierce through our own layers of apathy and cynicism – to hear that small inner voice, soothing yet challenging, calling through and beyond all humanity to inspire action rooted in caring about others. As we harness our inner power, we may meet an inner adversary: cowardice, propped up by a web of clever excuses. That is why we need to connect with our intuitive, spiritual strength to enable it to trump our fears. As we ready ourselves for action, we need to anchor our ego to the wisdom that informs our humility so that we will respect legitimate differences while acting on our universal humanity.

When our inner agency is allied with the action of other people committed to the just reconstruction of social relations themselves – then liberation is well on its way. This effort is undoubtedly a tall order; and yet at the same time it flows naturally from a commitment to honour the voices of people who have been silenced for too long. Social justice is therefore interconnected with participatory democracy. That is, social and economic and environmental justice demands a transformation of power, including a basic democratization of wealth-creating activities – so that the practice of authentic democracy comes within the reach of everyone rather than being manipulated by those who now dominate the heights of our economic, political, and social structures. That, then, is the challenge – for you, for me – not just for social service providers, but for everyone.

REFERENCES

Aboriginal Committee, Community Panel. 1992. *Liberating our children, liberating our nations.* Victoria: Family and Children's Services Legislation Review, Government of British Columbia.

Abramovitz, Mimi. 1988. *Regulating the lives of women: Social welfare policy from colonial times to the present.* Boston: South End Press.

Absolon, Kathy (Minogiizhigokwe). 2009. "Navigating the landscape of practice: Dbaagmowin of a helper." In *Wícihitowin: Aboriginal social work in Canada,* ed. Raven Sinclair (Ótiskewápíwskew), Michael Anthony Hart (Kaskitémahikan), and Gord Bruyere (Amawaajibitang). Black Point, N.S.: Fernwood Publishing.

Adams, J. Roy. 2009. "Collective bargaining is about a great deal more than money: Democracy is missing when 70% of workers lack basic rights." *CCPA Monitor,* 16 (4). Ottawa: Canadian Centre for Policy Alternatives.

Adamson, Nancy, Linda Briskin, and Margaret McPhail. 1988. *Feminist organizing for change: The contemporary women's movement in Canada.* Toronto: Oxford University Press.

Aging in Canada. 2010. "Alcohol and seniors: Lesbian, gay, bisexual and transgender (LGBT) older adults." ⟨http://www.agingincanada.ca/lgbt_older_adults.htm⟩.

Albert, Jim. 1991. "500 years of Indigenous survival and struggle." *Canadian Review of Social Policy,* 28.

Aleem, Rebecca. 2009. "The Human rights of girls in the criminal justice system of British Columbia: Realities and remedies." In *Justice system monitoring/Prisoner justice.* ⟨www.justiceforgirls.org⟩.

Alinsky, Saul D. 1946. *Reveille for radicals.* Chicago: University of Chicago.

Asmar, Christine and Page, Susan. 2009. "Sources of satisfaction and stress among Indigenous academic teachers: Findings from a national Australian study." *Asia Pacific Journal of Education,* 29(3).

Assembly of First Nations. 2004–2005. *A report card: Royal Commission on Aboriginal Peoples at 10 years.* ⟨www.afn.ca⟩.

Assembly of First Nations. 2010. "About AFN." ⟨www.afn.ca⟩.

Bailey, Gordon and Noga Gayle. 2003. *Ideology: Structuring identities in contemporary life.* Peterborough, Ont: Broadview Press, 2003.

Baines, Donna, ed. 2007a. *Doing anti-oppressive practice: Building transformative politicized social work.* Black Point, N.S.: Fernwood Publishing.

Baines, Donna. 2007b. "Anti-oppressive social work practice: Fighting for space, fighting for change." In *Doing anti-oppressive practice: Building transformative politicized social work*, ed. Donna Baines. Black Point, N.S.: Fernwood Publishing.

Baines, Donna. 2007c. "'If you could change one thing': Restructuring, social workers and social justice practice." In *Doing anti-oppressive practice: Building transformative politicized social work*, ed. Donna Baines. Black Point, N.S.: Fernwood Publishing.

Baines, Donna. 2007d. "Extending a radical tradition: Building transformative, politicized social work." In *Doing anti-oppressive practice: Building transformative politicized social work*, ed. Donna Baines. Black Point, N.S.: Fernwood Publishing.

Baines, T. Carol. 1998. "Women's professions and an ethic of care." In *Women's caring: Feminist perspectives on social welfare*, 2nd ed., ed. Carol T. Baines, Patricia M. Evans, and Sheila M. Neysmith. Toronto: Oxford University Press.

Bantjes, Rod. 2007. *Social movements in a global context: Canadian perspectives*. Toronto: Canadian Scholars' Press.

Barnes, Colin, Mike Oliver, and Len Barton. 2002. "Introduction." In *Disability studies today*, ed. Colin Barnes, Mike Oliver, and Len Barton. Cambridge: Polity Press.

Barnoff, Lisa. 2001. "Moving beyond words: Integrating anti-oppressive practice into feminist social service organizations." *Canadian Social Work Review*, 18(1).

Barnoff, Lisa. 2002. "New directions for anti-oppression practice in feminist social service agencies." Ph.D. thesis. Faculty of Social Work, University of Toronto.

Barrett, Betty Jo. 2009. "Is 'safety' dangerous? A critical examination of the classroom as safe space." Unpublished manuscript.

Baskin, Cyndy (On-koo-khag-kno kwe). 2009. "Evolution and revolutions: Healing approaches with Aboriginal adults." In *Wícihitowin: Aboriginal social work in Canada*, ed. Raven Sinclair (Ótiskewápíwskew), Michael Anthony Hart (Kaskitémahikan), and Gord Bruyere (Amawaajibitang). Black Point, N.S.: Fernwood Publishing.

Beaver, Elana. 2004. "Voices of youth in care: Reclaiming our stories; healing Aboriginal child welfare survivors," In *A Collection of memoirs, documentaries and writings*," CD co-ordinated by Rachel Kronick, Montreal, CKUT, Radio McGill, 2004, CD hour 4.

Bellamy, Don. 1965. "Social welfare in Canada." *Encyclopedia of social work*. New York: National Association of Social Workers.

Benjamin, Akua. 2007. "Doing anti-oppressive social work: The importance of resistance, history and strategy." In *Doing anti-oppressive practice: Building transformative politicized social work*, ed. Donna Baines. Black Point, N.S.: Fernwood Publishing.

Bernard, Wanda, Lydia Lucas-White, and Dorothy Moore. 1981. "Two hands tied behind her back: The dual negative status of 'minority group' women." Paper presented to Canadian Association of Schools of Social Work's Annual Conference, Dalhousie University, Halifax, June.

Bielmeier, George. 2002. "Social work and sexual diversity." In *Social work in Canada: An introduction*, ed. Steven Hick. Toronto: Thompson Educational Publishing.

Bishop, Anne. 2002. *Becoming an ally: Breaking the cycle of oppression in people.* 2nd ed. Halifax: Fernwood Publishing.

Bocking, Richard. 2003. "Reclaiming the commons: Corporatism, privatization drive enclosure of the commons." *CCPA Monitor,* 10(5). Ottawa: Canadian Centre for Policy Alternatives.

Brotman, Shari, Bill Ryan, Shannon Collins, Line Chamberland, Robert Cormier, Danielle Julien, Elizabeth Meyer, Allan Peterkin, and Brenda Richard. 2007. "Coming out to care: Caregivers of gay and lesbian seniors in Canada." *The Gerontologist,* 47(4).

Brown, Catrina. 2007. "Feminist therapy, violence, problem drinking and re-storying women's lives: Reconceptualizing anti-oppressive feminist therapy." In *Doing anti-oppressive practice: Building transformative politicized social work,* ed. Donna Baines. Black Point, N.S.: Fernwood Publishing.

Brown, Jason D. and David Hannis. 2008. *Community development in Canada.* Toronto: Pearson Education.

Brown, Marion, Brenda K. Richard, and Leighann Wichman. 2010. "The Promise and relevance of structural social work and practice with queer people and communities." In *Structural social work in action: Examples from practice*, ed. Steven F. Hick, Heather I. Peters, Tammy Corner, and Tracy London. Toronto: Canadian Scholars' Press.

Burgess, Christian. 1999. "Internal and external stress factors associated with identity development of transgendered youth." In *Social services with transgendered youth*, ed. Gerald Mallon. New York: Haworth Press.

Burrill, Anne and Heather I. Peters. 2010. "Community development and administration in the structural tradition: Mezzo and macro levels of practice." In *Structural social work in action: Examples from practice,* ed. Steven F. Hick, Heather I. Peters, Tammy Corner, and Tracy London. Toronto: Canadian Scholars' Press.

Burstow, Bonnie and Don Weitz, eds. 1988. *Shrink resistant: The struggle against psychiatry in Canada.* Vancouver: New Star Books.

Butler, Robert N. 2001. "Ageism." In *The encyclopedia of aging*, 3rd ed., vol.1 (A-L), ed. George L. Maddox. New York: Springer Publishing.

Cajete, Gregory. "Look to the mountain: Reflections on Indigenous ecology." In *A people's ecology: Explorations in sustainable living*, ed. Gregory Cajete. Santa Fe, N.M.: Clear Lights Publishers.

Callahan, Marilyn. 2004. "Chalk and cheese: Feminist thinking and policy-making." In *Connecting policy to practice in the human services*, ed. Brian Wharf and Brad McKenzie. Toronto: Oxford University Press.

Callahan, Marilyn and Karen Swift. 2006. "Back to the present: Rethinking risk assessment in child welfare." In *Canadian social policy: Issues and perspectives*, 4th ed., ed. Anne Westhues. Waterloo, Ont.: Wilfrid Laurier University Press.

Campbell, Bruce. 2009. "Economic downturn is already as bad as in the early 1930s." *CCPA Monitor*, 16(3). Ottawa: Canadian Centre for Policy Alternatives.

Campbell, Carolyn. 2002. "The Search for congruency: Developing strategies for anti-oppressive social work pedagogy." *Canadian Social Work Review*, 19(1).

Canada Without Poverty. 2009. *Poverty and parliament*. Ottawa. Summer.

Canadian Association for Social Work Education. 2008. "CASWE standards of accreditation." ⟨www.caswe-acfts.ca⟩.

Canadian Association for Social Work Education. 2009. Correspondence. Ottawa.

Canadian Association of Family Resource Programs. 2009. "E-Valuation: Summary of 2007–2008 survey results." ⟨www.frp.ca⟩.

Canadian Association of Social Workers. 1932. *Social Welfare*, 14(6) (March).

Canadian Association of Social Workers. 2003. *Child welfare project: Creating conditions for good practice*. Ottawa.

Canadian Association of Social Workers. 2009. Correspondence. Ottawa.

Canadian Association of Social Workers. 2010a. "CASW presents the social work profession: What is social work?" Ottawa ⟨www.casw-acts.ca⟩.

Canadian Association of Social Workers. 2010b. "CASW presents the social work profession: What social workers do." Ottawa. ⟨www.casw-acts.ca⟩.

Canadian Association of University Teachers. 2007. "Full-time community college career program enrolment by major discipline and field of study, 1999–2000." *CAUT almanac of post-secondary education 2007*. ⟨http://www.caut.ca/uploads/Almanach_2007.pdf⟩.

Canadian Association of University Teachers. 2009. "Sources of debt by level of education, 2007." *CAUT almanac of post-secondary education 2009–2010*. ⟨http://www.caut.ca/pages.asp?page=442⟩.

Canadian Council of Chief Executives. 2010. "About CCCE." ⟨www.ceocouncil.ca⟩.

Canadian Council of Chief Executives. 2009. "CEO Council chief executive outlines key short-term and long-term priorities for Canada." ⟨www.ceocouncil.ca⟩. January.

Canadian Feminist Alliance for International Action and Canadian Labour Congress. 2010. "Reality check: Women in Canada and the Beijing Declaration and Platform for Action fifteen years on." *Publications*. ⟨http://www.canadianlabour.ca⟩.

Canadian Network for the Prevention of Elder Abuse. 2009. "What is ageism?" ⟨www.cnpea.ca/ageism.pdf⟩.

Canadian Social Research Links. 2009. "Key provincial and territorial government welfare links." ⟨http://www.canadiansocialresearch.net/welref.htm⟩.

Canadian Social Research Links. 2009. ⟨http://www.canadiansocialresearch
.net/welfare.htm⟩.

Capen Reynolds, Bertha. 1951. "Social work and social living: Explorations
in philosophy and practice." *Classics Series 1975, 1987*. Silver Spring,
Md.: National Association of Social Workers.

Carniol, Ben. 1992. "Structural social work: Maurice Moreau's challenge to
social work practice." *Journal of Progressive Human Services, 3(1)*.

Carniol, Ben. 2005a. "Structural social work (Canada)." In *Encyclopedia of
social welfare history*, ed. John M. Herrick and Paul H Stuart. Thousand
Oaks, Cal.: Sage Publications.

Carniol, Ben. 2005b. "Analysis of social location and change: Practice implications," in *Social work: A critical turn*, ed. Steven F. Hick, Jan Fook, and
Richard Pozzuto. Toronto: Thompson Educational Publishing.

Carniol, Ben and Vivian Del Valle. 2010. "'We have a voice': Helping immi-
grant women challenge abuse." In *Structural social work in action:
Examples from practice*, ed. Steven F. Hick, Heather I. Peters, Tammy
Corner, and Tracy London. Toronto: Canadian Scholars' Press.

Carniol, Naomi. 2004. "Still reaching out after all these years: Yellow Door
celebrates 100th anniversary." *The Gazette* (Montreal), June 7.

Centre for Suicide Prevention. 2003. "Suicide among gay, lesbian, bisexual or
transgendered youth." In *SIEC Alert no. 53*. Calgary: Canadian Mental
Health Association.

Child Care Information Hamilton. 2009. "Canadian Association of Family
Resource Programs." ⟨www.inform.hamilton.ca/record/HAM6171?Use-
CICvw=70⟩.

Child Poverty Action Network. 2009. "Child poverty quotes." ⟨www.renfrew-
countycpan.ca/child-poverty-quotes.cfm⟩.

Clarke, Janet L. 2003. "Reconceptualizing empathy for anti-oppressive, culturally competent practice." In *Emerging perspectives on anti-oppressive
practice*, ed. Wes Shera. Toronto: Canadian Scholars' Press.

Clews, Rosemary, William Randall, and Dolores Furlong. 2005. "Research
notes on interdisciplinary stories by rural helpers." In *Rural social work,
special issue on "Beyond disciplinary and geographical boundaries,"* 9(1).

Coates, John. 2003. *Towards a new paradigm*. Halifax: Fernwood Publishing.

Cohen, Erminie Joy. 1997. *Sounding the alarm: Poverty in Canada*. Ottawa:
Senate of Canada.

Cole-Arnal, Oscar. 1998. *To set the captives free: Liberation theology in
Canada*. Toronto: Between the Lines.

Copp, Terry. 1974. *The Anatomy of poverty: The condition of the working class
in Montreal 1907–1929*. Toronto: McClelland and Stewart.

Corrigan, Philip and Val Corrigan. 1980. "State formation and social policy
until 1871." In *Social work, welfare and the state*, ed. Noel Parry, Michael
Rustin, and Carol Satyamurti. Beverly Hills, Cal.: Sage.

Council of Canadians. 2010. "About us." ⟨www.canadians.org⟩.

Cram, Patricia Ellen. 2004. "Child protection work: An inside look." Master of social work thesis, Faculty of Social Work, University of Regina, Saskatchewan.

Curry-Stevens, Ann. 2009. "When economic growth doesn't trickle down: The wage dimensions of income polarization." In *Social determinants of health: Canadian perspectives*, 2nd ed., ed. Dennis Raphael. Toronto: Canadian Scholars' Press.

Cygman, Samara. 2004. "Fight continues for abused and neglected." *Cochrane Times* ⟨www.cochranetimes.com⟩, Sept. 29.

Dale, Jennifer and Peggy Foster. 1986. *Feminists and state welfare.* London: Routledge & Kegan Paul.

Daly, Mary. 1978. *Gyn/Ecology: The metaethics of radical feminism.* Boston: Beacon Press.

Davies, James B., Susanna Sandström, Anthony Shorrocks, and Edward N. Wolff. 2008. "The World distribution of household wealth." *Discussion Paper No. 2008/03.* Helsinki: World Institute for Development, United Nations University. February.

Davidson, Carl. 2010. "U.S. Steelworkers plan to experiment with factory ownership: Union to link with Mondragon worker cooperative movement." *CCPA Monitor*, 16 (8). Ottawa: Canadian Centre for Policy Alternatives.

de Schweinitz, Karl. 1943. *England's road to social security.* New York: Barnes.

Dominelli, Lena and Ankie Hoogvelt. 1996. "Globalization and the technocratization of social work." *Critical Social Policy,* 16(47).

Dua, Enakshi. 1999. "Beyond diversity: Exploring the ways in which the discourse of race has shaped the institution of the nuclear family." In *Scratching the surface: Canadian anti-racist feminist thought*, ed. Enakshi Dua and Angela Robertson. Toronto: Women's Press.

Dunn, Peter A. 2003. "Canadians with disabilities." In *Canadian social policy: Issues and perspectives*, ed. Anne Westhues. Waterloo, Ont.: Wilfrid Laurier University Press.

Dunn, Peter A. 2006. "Canadians with disabilities." In *Canadian social policy: Issues and perspectives,* 4th ed., ed. Anne Westhues. Waterloo, Ont.: Wilfrid Laurier University Press.

Dumbrill, Gary, and Winnie Lo. 2009. "What parents say: Service users' theory and anti-oppressive child welfare practice." In *Walking this path together: Anti-racist and anti-oppressive child welfare practice,* ed. Susan Strega and Sohki Aski Esquao (Jeannine Carrière). Black Point, N.S.: Fernwood Publishing.

Eldridge v. British Columbia (A.G.). 1997. 3 S.C.R. 624.

Elliott, Larry. 2004. "Pursuit of 'job flexibility' a dubious route to full employment." *CCPA Monitor,* 11(2). Ottawa: Canadian Centre for Policy Alternatives.

Equity Office of the University of British Columbia. 2010. "Terminology." *Positive Space Campaign* ⟨www.positivespace.ubc.ca/⟩.

Feehan, Richard, Maureen Boettcher, and Kathaleen S. Quinn. 2010. "The societal context of child sexual abuse." In *Structural social work in action: Examples from practice,* ed. Steven F. Hick, Heather I. Peters, Tammy Corner, and Tracy London. Toronto: Canadian Scholars' Press.

Ferguson, Iain. 2008. *Reclaiming social work.* London: Sage Publications.

Findlay, Peter. 1982. "The 'Welfare State' and the state of welfare in Canada." Paper presented at annual conference of Canadian Association of Schools of Social Work. Ottawa.

Finkel, Alvin. 1977. "Origins of the welfare state in Canada." In *The Canadian state: political economy and political power,* ed. Leo Panitch. Toronto: University of Toronto Press.

Finley, Judy, 2004. "Voices of youth in care: Interview of Ontario's Chief Advocate for the Rights of the Child." In *A Collection of memoirs, documentaries and writings,* CD co-ordinated by Rachel Kronick, Montreal, CKUT, Radio McGill, 2004, CD hour 4.

First Nations Child and Family Caring Society of Canada. 2010. "I am a witness: Why is this case important?" ⟨www.fnwitness.ca⟩.

Freeman, Bonnie. 2007. "Indigenous pathways to anti-oppressive practice." In *Doing anti-oppressive practice: Building transformative politicized social work,* ed. Donna Baines. Black Point, N.S.: Fernwood Publishing.

Frosst, Sandra with assistance from Gwyn Frayne, Mary Hlywa, Lynne Leonard, Marilyn Rowell. 1993. *Empowerment II: Snapshots of the structural approach.* Ottawa: Carleton University.

Gauci, Rosemary, Emelyn Bartlett, and Colleen Grey. 2004. "Focus on the special needs of youth and their families." *Mental Health Matters,* Spring edition. Toronto Branch: Canadian Mental Health Association.

George, Purnima. 2003. "Going beyond the superficial: Capturing structural social work practice." In *Research report.* Toronto: School of Social Work, Ryerson University.

George, Purnima. 2004. "Structural social work practice in Toronto agencies: The perspective of service users." Paper at Conference of the Canadian Association of Schools of Social Work. Winnipeg, June.

George, Purnima, Brienne Coleman, and Lisa Barnoff. 2007. "Beyond 'providing services': Voices of service users on structural social work practice in community-based social service agencies." *Canadian Social Work Review,* 24 (1).

Germain, Carel B. and Alex Gitterman. 1980. *The life model of social work practice.* New York: Columbia University Press.

Goar, Carol. 2010. "Historic moment for nation's disabled." *Toronto Star,* March 17, A15.

Gosine, Kevin and Gordon Pon. 2010. "On the front lines: The voices and experiences of racialized child welfare workers in Ontario." Paper presented at the meeting of the Canadian Sociological Association, Montreal.

Graveline, Fyre Jean. 1998. *Circle works: Transforming Eurocentric consciousness.* Halifax: Fernwood Publishing.

Griffin Cohen, Marjorie. 2009. "Response to the recession: Rescue the economy, protect people, and plan for the future." *CCPA Monitor,* 16(1). Ottawa: Canadian Centre for Policy Alternatives.

Grossman, Richard. 2010. "Challenging corporate rule: Companies should bow to people, not people to companies." *CCPA Monitor,* 16 (8). Ottawa: Canadian Centre for Policy Alternatives.

Guest, Dennis. 1980. *The Emergence of social security in Canada.* Vancouver: University of British Columbia.

Guest, Dennis. 1985. "Social security." In *Canadian encyclopedia.* Edmonton: Hurtig.

Hanes, Roy. 2006. "Social work with persons with disabilities: Helping individuals and their families." In *Social work in Canada: An introduction,* 2nd ed., ed. Steve F. Hick. Toronto: Thompson Educational Publishing.

Hart, Michael Anthony (Kaskitémahikan). 2009a. "For Indigenous people, by Indigenous people, with Indigenous people: Towards an Indigenous research paradigm." In *Wícihitowin: Aboriginal social work in Canada,* ed. Raven Sinclair (Ótiskewápíwskew), Michael Anthony Hart (Kaskitémahikan), and Gord Bruyere (Amawaajibitang). Black Point, N.S.: Fernwood Publishing.

Hart, Michael Anthony (Kaskitémahikan). 2009b. "Anti-colonial Indigenous social work reflections on an Aboriginal approach." In *Wícihitowin: Aboriginal social work in Canada,* ed. Raven Sinclair (Ótiskewápíwskew), Michael Anthony Hart (Kaskitémahikan), and Gord Bruyere (Amawaajibitang). Black Point, N.S.: Fernwood Publishing.

Hashemi, Nader. July 14. 2009. "Grand Ayatollah Hossein-Ali Montazeri: System based on force illegitimate." ⟨www.therealnews.com⟩.

Heinonen, Tuula and Len Spearman. 2001. *Social work practice: Problem-solving and beyond.* Toronto/Vancouver: Irwin.

Hemingway, Dawn, Clarie Johnson, and Brenda Roland. 2010. "Addressing the immediate needs of service users as part of fundamental structural change: Complementary or contradictory processes?" In *Structural social work in action: Examples from practice,* ed. Steven F. Hick, Heather I. Peters, Tammy Corner, and Tracy London. Toronto: Canadian Scholars' Press.

Henry, Frances and Carol Tator. 2006. *The Colour of democracy: Racism in Canadian society.* 3rd ed. Toronto: Thompson Nelson.

Herbert, Margot. 2003. *Child welfare project: Creating conditions for good practice.* Ottawa: Canadian Association of Social Workers.

Hick, Steven F. 2006. *Social work in Canada: An introduction.* 2nd ed. Toronto: Thompson Educational Publishing.

Hick, Steven F., Heather I. Peters, Tammy Corner, and Tracy London, eds.

2010. *Structural social work in action: Examples from practice.* Toronto: Canadian Scholars' Press.

Honderich, John. 2003. "Star's statistics analysis holds up to fair scrutiny." *Toronto Star,* March 1.

hooks, bell. 2003. *Teaching community: A pedagogy of hope.* New York: Routledge.

House of Commons, Canada. 1983. *Minutes of the proceedings of the Special Committee on Indian Self-Government,* 40, Oct. 12, Oct. 20.

House of Commons. 2008. *Debates: Official report (Hansard).* Vol.142, No. 110, 2nd session, 28th Parliament, June 11. ⟨www2.parl.gc.ca/housechamberbusiness/chambersittings.aspx⟩.

Hudema, Mike. 2004. *An Action a day keeps global capitalism away.* Toronto: Between the Lines, 2004.

Hulko, Wendy. 2009. "The Time- and context-contingent nature of intersectionality and interlocking oppressions." *Affilia,* 24(1).

Human Resources and Social Development Canada. 2006. Federal-Territorial-Provincial Directors of Income Support. "Social assistance statistical report 2005." ⟨www.sdc.gc.ca/en/cs/sp/sdc/socpol/page00.shtml⟩.

Human Skills Development Canada. 2008. Workplace Information, Labour Program. "Union membership in Canada – 2007." ⟨http://www.rhdcc-hrsdc.gc.ca/eng/lp/wid/union_membership.shtml⟩.

Indigenous Peoples Issues and Resources. 2010. "About Us/Indigenous peoples issues & resources sitemap/ Indigenous peoples: Resources / Graduate programs." ⟨www.indigenouspeoplesissues.com⟩.

Inuit Tapiriit Kanatami. 2010. "About ITK." ⟨www.itk.ca⟩.

Irving, Allan. 1981. "Canadian fabians: The work and thought of Harry Cassidy and Leonard Marsh, 1930–1945." *Canadian Journal of Social Work Education,* 7(1).

Irving, Allan. 1989. "'The Master principle of administering relief': Jeremy Bentham, Sir Francis Bond Head and the establishment of the principle of less eligibility in Upper Canada." *Canadian Review of Social Policy,* 23 (May).

Jeffery, Donna. 2009. "Meeting here and now: Reflections on racial and cultural difference in social work encounters." In *Walking this path together: Anti-racist and anti-oppressive child welfare practice,* ed. Susan Strega and Sohki Aski Esquao (Jeannine Carrière). Black Point, N.S.: Fernwood Publishing.

Justice for Girls. 2003. "Young women in prison speak out." In *Publications and positions.* ⟨www.justiceforgirls.org⟩.

Kenyon, Gail L. 2003. "Does he always get to be the boy? Examining the gender gap in social work." *Canadian Social Work Review,* 20(2).

Kinewesquao [Richardson, Cathy]. 2009. "Métis experiences of social work practice." In *Walking this path together: Anti-racist and anti-oppressive child welfare practice,* ed. Susan Strega and Sohki Aski Esquao (Jeannine Carrière). Black Point, N.S.: Fernwood Publishing.

Kinewesquao [Richardson, Cathy] and Wade, Allan. 2009. "Taking resistance seriously: A response-based approach to social work in cases of violence against Indigenous women." In *Walking this path together: Anti-racist and anti-oppressive child welfare practice,* ed. Susan Strega and Sohki Aski Esquao (Jeannine Carrière). Black Point, N.S.: Fernwood Publishing.

Kivel, Paul. 1996. *Uprooting racism: How white people can work for racial justice.* Philadelphia: New Society.

Klein, Naomi. 2008. *The shock doctrine: The rise of disaster capitalism.* Toronto: Random House.

Klein, Seth and Yalnizyan, Armine. 2010. "Reducing poverty, inequality will spur economic recovery." *CCPA Monitor,* 16(9). Ottawa: Canadian Centre for Policy Alternatives.

Kumsa, Martha Kuwee. 2007. "A Settlement story of unsettlement: Transformative practices of taking it personally." In *Doing anti-oppressive practice: Building transformative politicized social work,* ed. Donna Baines. Black Point, N.S.: Fernwood Publishing.

LaBerge, Roy. 2010. "New economy is needed to replace failed neoliberal system: Book review of Beyond the bubble: Imagining a new Canadian economy by James Laxer." *CCPA Monitor,* 16(9). Ottawa: Canadian Centre for Policy Alternatives.

La Rose, Tara. 2009. "One small revolution: Unionization, community practice, and workload in child welfare." *Journal of Community Practice,* 17(1).

Ladd, Deena and Trish Hennessy. 2009. "New labour: When workers unite for fair treatment – how to rid the uneasy world of part-time work of unfairness, low pay and exploitation." *Toronto Star,* July 11.

Laird, Joan. 1995. "Family-centered practice: Feminist, constructionist, and cultural perspectives." In *Feminist practice in the 21st Century,* ed. Nan Van Den Bergh. Washington: National Association of Social Work Press.

Lappin, Bernard. 1965. "Stages in the development of community organization work as a social work method." Ph.D. dissertation. School of Social Work, University of Toronto.

Latta, Ruth. 2009. "More equal societies do better: The bigger the income gap, the worse the social problems." *CCPA Monitor,* 16(2). Ottawa: Canadian Centre for Policy Alternatives.

Lavallée, Lynn F. 2008. "Balancing the Medicine Wheel through physical activity." *Journal of Aboriginal Health.* January. ⟨http://www.naho.ca/english/journal/jah04_01/09MedicineWheel_64–71.pdf⟩.

Lavallée, Lynn F. 2009a. "Practical application of an Indigenous research framework and two qualitative Indigenous research methods: Sharing circles and Anishnaabe symbol-based reflection." *International Journal of Qualitative Methods,* 8(1).

Lavallée, Lynn F. 2009b. "Evaluation of culture camp: First Nations Technical

Institute - Ryerson University Bachelor of Social Work Programme."
Toronto: School of Social Work, Ryerson University.

Lavallée, Lynn F. and Jennifer M. Poole. 2009. "Beyond recovery: Colonization, health and healing for Indigenous people in Canada." *International
Journal of Mental Health Addiction*, 8(1).

League for Human Rights of B'nai Brith. 2009. "Audit of anti-Semitic incidents: Patterns of Prejudice in Canada." ⟨www.bnaibrith.ca⟩.

Lee, Bill and Sarah Todd. 2007. *A Casebook of community practice: Problems
and strategies*. Mississauga, Ont.: Common Act Press.

Lee, Marc. 2004. "Size of government and economic performance: What
does the evidence say?" In *Behind the Numbers: Economic Facts, Figures
and Analysis, CCPA Monitor*, 6(2). B.C. Office of the Canadian Centre for
Policy Alternatives.

Levine, Helen. 1982. "The personal is political: Feminism and the helping
professions." In *Feminism in Canada: From pressure to politics*, ed.
Angela R. Miles and Geraldine Finn. Montreal: Black Rose Books.

Lightman, Ernie. 2003. *Social policy in Canada*. Toronto: Oxford University
Press.

Lindert, Peter. 2004. *Growing public: Social spending and economic growth
since the eighteenth century*. Cambridge University Press, quoted in Lee,
"Size of government and economic performance: What does the evidence say?" In *Behind the Numbers: Economic Facts, Figures and Analysis, CCPA Monitor*, 6(2). B.C. Office of the Canadian Centre for Policy
Alternatives.

London, Tracy. (2009). "Mindfulness and activism: Fighting for justice as a
self-reflective emancipatory practice." In *Mindfulness and social work*,
ed. Steven F. Hick. Chicago: Lyceum Books.

Lubove, Roy. 1965. *Professional altruist*. Boston: Harvard University Press.

Lundy, Colleen. 2004. *Social work and social justice: A Structural approach to
practice*. Peterborough, Ont.: Broadview Press.

Lysack, Mishka. 2010. "Practice and skills for building social and ecological
resiliency with individuals and communities." In *Structural social work
in action: Examples from practice*, ed. Steven F. Hick, Heather I. Peters,
Tammy Corner, and Tracy London. Toronto: Canadian Scholars' Press.

Macarov, David. 1978. *The Design of social welfare*. New York: Holt, Rinehart
& Winston.

MacDonald, Judy E. and Gaila Friars. 2010. "Structural social work from a
(dis)Ability perspective." In *Structural social work in action: Examples
from practice*, ed. Steven F. Hick, Heather I. Peters, Tammy Corner, and
Tracy London. Toronto: Canadian Scholars' Press.

Mackenzie, Hugh. 2007. "Editorial: The rich are getting richer – and we're
all helping," *CCPA Monitor*, October. ⟨www.policyalternatives.ca/Editori-
als/2007/10/Editorial1724/⟩.

Madison, Nora, 2009. "Abstract: Fluid identity and embodied selves: Virtual
community and the narratives of bisexuality in online social networking

sites." *Open conference systems, Internet research 10.0.*⟨http://ocs.sfu.ca/aoir/index.php/ir/10/paper/view/335⟩.

Mallon, Gerald P. 1999. "Practice with transgendered children" In *Social services with transgendered youth*, ed. Gerald Mallon. New York: Haworth Press.

Marcus, S. 1978. "Their brothers' keepers." In *Doing good: The limits of benevolence*, ed. Willard Gaylin. New York: Pantheon.

McGill University Equity Subcommittee on Queer People. 2010. "Recognizing heterosexism and homophobia: Creating an anti-heterosexist, homophobia-free campus." ⟨www.mcgill.ca/queerequity/heterosexism/⟩.

McIntosh, Peggy. 1998. "White privilege: Unpacking the invisible knapsack." In *Re-visioning family therapy: Race, culture and gender in clinical practice*, ed. Monica McGoldrick. New York: Guilford.

McIntosh, Peggy. 2007. "White privilege and male privilege: A personal account of coming to see correspondence through work in women's studies." In *Intersections of gender, race and class: Readings for a changing landscape*, ed. Marcia Texler Segal and Theresa A. Martinez. Los Angeles: Roxbury Publishing.

McKenzie, Hugh. 2010. "Debate over taxes dangerously one-sided and misleading." *CCPA Monitor*, 16 (8). Ottawa: Canadian Centre for Policy Alternatives.

McMullin, Julie. 2004. *Understanding social inequality: Intersections of class, age, gender, ethnicity, and race in Canada.* Toronto: Oxford University Press.

McMurtry, John. 2009. "Taxation and poverty: Injustice built into our tax system hurts poor the most." *CCPA Monitor,* 16(2). Ottawa: Canadian Centre for Policy Alternatives.

McQuaig, Linda. 2001. *All you can eat: Greed, lust and the new capitalism.* Toronto: Penguin.

Métis National Council. 2010. "Métis rights." ⟨www.metisnation.ca⟩.

Meyer-Cook, Fiona and Diane Labelle. 2004. "Namaji: Two-Spirit organizing in Montreal, Canada." *Journal of Gay and Lesbian Social Service: Issues in Practice, Policy and Research,* 6(1).

Moran, Bridget. 1992. *A little rebellion.* Vancouver: Arsenal Pulp Press.

Morissette, René and Xuelin Zhang. 2006. "Revisiting wealth inequality." *Perspective,* No. 14, Catalogue no. 75–001-XIE. Ottawa: Statistics Canada. ⟨http://www.statcan.gc.ca⟩.

Morrisseau, Calvin. 1999. *Into the daylight: A wholistic approach to healing.* Toronto: University of Toronto Press.

Moscovitch, Allan. 1986. "The welfare state since 1975." *Journal of Canadian Studies,* 21(2).

Mullaly, Bob. 2010. *Challenging oppression and confronting privilege: A Critical social work approach.* 2nd ed. Toronto: Oxford University Press.

Murphy, Yvette, Valerie Hunt, Anna M. Zajicek, Adele N. Norris, and Leah Hamilton. 2009. *Incorporating intersectionality in social work practice, research, policy and education.* Washington: National Association of Social Workers Press.

Murray, Kate M. and Steven F. Hick. 2010. "Structural social work: Theory and process." In *Structural social work in action: Examples from practice,* ed. Steven F. Hick, Heather I. Peters, Tammy Corner, and Tracy London. Toronto: Canadian Scholars' Press.

Nakata, Martin. 2004. "Ongoing conversations about Aboriginal and Torres Strait Islander research agendas and directions." *Australian Journal of Indigenous Education,* 33.

National Anti-Racism Council of Canada. 2007. "Racial discrimination in Canada: Submissions to the Committee on the Elimination of All Forms of Racial Discrimination on the occasion of the review of Canada's seventeenth and eighteenth reports on the United Nations under the International Convention on the Elimination of All Forms of Racial Discrimination." *Campaigns and projects.* Toronto. ⟨www.narcc.ca⟩.

National Council of Welfare. 2004. "Press release: Welfare incomes 2003." July 7. ⟨http://www.canadiansocialresearch.net/welref.htm⟩.

National Council of Welfare. 2008. Release of welfare incomes. ⟨www.ncwc-nbes.net⟩.

Neysmith, Sheila. 2006. "Caring and aging." In *Canadian social policy: Issues and perspectives,* ed. Anne Westhues. 4th ed. Waterloo, Ont.: Wilfrid Laurier University Press.

Nhat Hanh, Thich. 1991. *Peace is every step: The path of mindfulness in everyday life.* New York: Bantam.

O'Brien, Mary. 1982. "Feminist praxis." In *Feminism in Canada: From pressure to politics,* ed. Angela R. Miles and Geraldine Finn. Montreal: Black Rose Books.

Office of the United Nations High Commissioner for Human Rights. 2009. "International covenant on economic, social and cultural rights." Articles 9 and 11. ⟨http://www2.ohchr.org/english/law/cescr.htm⟩.

Okasha, Samir. 2008. "Biological altruism." In *The Stanford encyclopedia of philosophy,* ed. Edward N. Zalta ⟨http://plato.stanford.edu/entries/altruism-biological⟩.

Olivier, Claude. 2010. "Operationalizing structural theory: Guidelines for practice." In *Structural social work in action: Examples from practice,* ed. Steven F. Hick, Heather I. Peters, Tammy Corner, and Tracy London. Toronto: Canadian Scholars' Press.

O'Neill, Brian. 2006. "Toward inclusion of gay and lesbian people: Social policy changes in relation to sexual orientation." In *Canadian social policy: Issues and perspectives,* 4th ed., ed. Anne Westhues. Waterloo Ont.: Wilfrid Laurier University Press.

Ordre professionnel des travailleurs sociaux du Québec. 2009. "Rapport annuel 2008–2009: Les Statistiques." ⟨www.optsq.org⟩.

Parada, Henry. 2009. "Reconstructing neglect and emotional maltreatment from an anti-oppressive perspective." In *Walking this path together: Anti-*

racist and anti-oppressive child welfare practice, ed. Susan Strega and Sohki Aski Esquao (Jeannine Carrière). Black Point, N.S.: Fernwood Publishing.

Paris, Erna. 1995. *The end of days: Tolerance, tyranny and the expulsion of Jews from Spain.* Toronto: Lester Publishing.

Payne, Malcolm Stuart. 1997. *Modern social work theory,* 2nd ed. Chicago: Lyceum Books.

Peters, Heather I., Tracy London, Tammy Corner, and Steven F. Hick. 2010. "Concluding thoughts and future directions." In *Structural social work in action: Examples from practice,* ed. Steven F. Hick, Heather I. Peters, Tammy Corner, and Tracy London. Toronto: Canadian Scholars' Press.

Peters, Heather I. 2010. "Situating practitioners' experiences in a model of theory-practice integration." In *Structural social work in action: Examples from practice,* ed. Steven F. Hick, Heather I. Peters, Tammy Corner, and Tracy London. Toronto: Canadian Scholars' Press.

Pillari, Vimala. 2002. *Social work practice: Theories and skills.* Boston: Allyn and Bacon.

Piven, Frances Fox and Richard A. Cloward. 1979. *Poor peoples' movements: Why they succeed, how they fail.* New York: Vintage Books.

Popple, B. 1983. "Contexts of practice." In *Handbook of clinical social work,* ed. A. Rosenblatt and D. Waldvogel. San Francisco: Jossey Bass.

Porter, Beth. 2010. "Invited into understanding: An interview with AFN National Chief Shawn A-in-chut Atleo." *A Human Future,* 9(1). Toronto: L'Arche Canada. ⟨www.larche.ca/en/inspiration/⟩.

Rabbis for Human Rights. 2010. "About RHR." ⟨www.rhr.org.il/index.php ?language=en⟩.

Rabble. 2009. "About us." ⟨www.rabble.ca⟩.

Razack, Narda and Donna Jeffery. 2002. "Critical race discourse and tenets for social work." *Canadian Social Work Review,* 19(2).

Real News Network, The. 2010. "About us." ⟨http://therealnews.com/t/⟩.

Rebick, Judy. 2009. *Transforming power: From the personal to the political.* Toronto: Penguin Canada.

Riches, Graham. 2004. "Right to food: Case study – Canada." Paper for the International Working Group for the Elaboration of a Set of Voluntary Guidelines to Support the Progressive Realization of the Right to Adequate Food in the Context of National Food Security. Rome: Food and Agricultural Organization, United Nations.

Riley, Barbara (Waubauno Kwe). 1994. "Teachings from the Medicine Wheel: Theories for practice." WUNSKA Network Presentation: Annual Conference of Canadian Association of Schools of Social Work, Calgary, June 16.

Ross, David P., Katherine J. Scott, and Peter J. Smith. 2000. *The Canadian fact book on poverty.* Ottawa: Canadian Council on Social Development. ⟨www.ccsd.ca⟩.

Rothman, Laurel. 2009. "Family security in insecure times: The case for a poverty reduction strategy for Canada." News Release of Presentation to

Federal Government on 2009 Pre-Budget Consultation. Toronto. Jan. 8 ⟨www.campaign2000.ca⟩.

Royal Commission on Aboriginal Peoples. 1996. *Looking forward, looking back: Report of the Royal Commission on Aboriginal Peoples.* Vol. 1. Ottawa: Minister of Supply and Services Canada.

Saulis, Malcolm A. 2006. "Program and policy development from a holistic Aboriginal perspective." In *Canadian social policy: Issues and perspectives*, 4th ed., ed. Anne Westhues. Waterloo, Ont.: Wilfrid Laurier University Press.

Sauvé, Julie and Mike Burns. May 2009. "Residents of Canada's shelters for abused women, 2008." *Juristat*, (29)2. ⟨www.statcan.gc.ca⟩.

Schouls, Tim, John Olthuis, and Diane Engelstad. 1992. "The basic dilemma: Sovereignty or assimilation." In *Nation to nation: Aboriginal sovereignty and the future of Canada*, ed. Diane Engelstad and John Bird. Concord, Ont.: Anansi.

Schwartz, Karen and Ann-Marie O'Brien. 2010. "Injustice can happen whether you're psychotic or not: Incorporating structural social work theory in a mental health setting." In *Structural social work in action: Examples from practice*, ed. Steven F. Hick, Heather I. Peters, Tammy Corner, and Tracy London. Toronto: Canadian Scholars' Press.

Scott, Katherine. 2009. Social development report series. Ottawa: Canadian Council on Social Development. ⟨http://www.ccsd.ca⟩.

Seebaran, Roop. 2003. "A Community approach to combating racism." In *Emerging perspectives on anti-oppressive practice*, ed. Wes Shera. Toronto: Canadian Scholars' Press.

Shapcott, Michael. 2009. "Housing." In *Social determinants of health: Canadian perspectives*, 2nd ed., ed. Dennis Raphael. Toronto: Canadian Scholars' Press.

Shiva, Vandana 2002. "Preface." In *Water wars: Privatization, pollution and profit.* Toronto: Between the Lines.

Silver, Susan, Rachel Berman, and Sue Wilson. 2005. "A place to go . . . : Stories from participants of Family Resource Programs." MAFRP – Ryerson University project ⟨www.ryerson.ca/voices⟩.

Sinclair, Raven (Ótiskewápíwskew). 2009a. "Identity or racism? Aboriginal transracial adoption." In *Wícihitowin: Aboriginal social work in Canada*, ed. Raven Sinclair (Ótiskewápíwskew), Michael Anthony Hart (Kaskitémahikan), and Gord Bruyere (Amawaajibitang). Black Point, N.S.: Fernwood Publishing.

Sinclair, Raven (Ótiskewápíwskew). 2009b. "Bridging the past and the future." In *Wícihitowin: Aboriginal social work in Canada*, ed. Raven Sinclair (Ótiskewápíwskew), Michael Anthony Hart (Kaskitémahikan), and Gord Bruyere (Amawaajibitang). Black Point, N.S.: Fernwood Publishing.

Sinclair, Raven (Ótiskewápíwskew), Michael Anthony Hart (Kaskitémahikan), and Gord Bruyere (Amawaajibitang), eds. 2009. *Wícihitowin: Aboriginal social work in Canada.* Black Point, N.S.: Fernwood Publishing.

Smith, Jackie. 2008. *Social movements for global democracy.* Baltimore: Johns Hopkins University Press.

Snyder, Linda. 2006. "Workfare: Ten years of pickin' on the poor." In *Canadian social policy: Issues and perspectives*, 4th ed., ed. Anne Westhues. Waterloo, Ont.: Wilfrid Laurier University Press.

Social Work Action Network. 2010. "Social work and social justice: A manifesto for a new engaged practice." ⟨www.socialworkfuture.org/?_id=50⟩.

Special Senate Committee on Aging. 2009. *Final report: Canada's aging population: Seizing the opportunity.* Ottawa. ⟨www.senate-senat.ca/age.ascitation⟩.

Special Senate Committee on Poverty. 1971. *Poverty in Canada.* Ottawa: Information Canada

Spivey, Donald. 2003. *Fire from the soul: A History of the African-American struggle.* Durham, N.C.: Carolina Academic Press.

Stephenson, Marylee, Gilles Rondeau, Jean Claude Michaud, and Sid Fiddler. 2001. *In Critical demand: Social work in Canada: Final report.* Vol. 1. Ottawa: Human Resources Development Canada, Canadian Association of Schools of Social Work, Canadian Committee of Deans and Directors of Schools of Social Work, Canadian Association of Social Workers, and Regroupement des Unités de formation universitaires en travail social.

Sterling-Collins, Rona (Quistaletko). 2009. "A holistic approach to supporting children with special needs." In *Wícihitowin: Aboriginal social work in Canada,* ed. Raven Sinclair (Ótiskewápíwskew), Michael Anthony Hart (Kaskitémahikan), and Gord Bruyere (Amawaajibitang). Black Point, N.S.: Fernwood Publishing.

Steven, Peter. 2004. *The No-nonsense guide to global media.* Toronto: Between the Lines.

Strega, Susan and Sohki Aski Esquao (Jeannine Carrière). 2009. "Introduction." In *Walking this path together: Anti-racist and anti-oppressive child welfare practice*, ed. Susan Strega and Sohki Aski Esquao (Jeannine Carrière). Black Point, N.S.: Fernwood Publishing.

Strega, Susan. 2009. "Anti-oppressive approaches to assessment, risk assessment and file recording." In *Walking this path together: Anti-racist and anti-oppressive child welfare practice*, ed. Susan Strega and Sohki Aski Esquao (Jeannine Carrière). Black Point, N.S.: Fernwood Publishing.

Strojeck, Sylvia. 2008. "From East to West: Tears, applause and defiance greet Ottawa's gesture." *Toronto Star*, June 12.

Struthers, James. 1983. *No fault of their own: Unemployment and the Canadian welfare state, 1914–1941.* Toronto: University of Toronto Press.

Swan, Tracy A. 2002. "Coming out and self-disclosure: Exploring the pedagogical significance in teaching social work students about homophobia and heterosexism." *Canadian Social Work Review,* 19(1).

Swanson, Jean. 2001, *Poor-bashing: The politics of exclusion.* Toronto: Between the Lines.

Swift, Jamie, Jacqueline M. Davies, Robert G. Clarke, and Michael Czerny

S.J. 2003. *Getting started on social analysis in Canada.* 4th ed. Toronto: Between the Lines.

Taskforce on Anti-Racism at Ryerson. 2010. *Final Report.* Toronto: Ryerson University.

Texler Segal, Marcia and Theresa A. Martinez, eds. 2007. *Intersections of gender, race and class: Readings for a changing landscape.* Los Angeles: Roxbury Publishing.

Thakur, Ramesh. 2004. "Why we shouldn't rush to war over Darfur." *The Globe and Mail,* Sept. 11.

Thomas Bernard, Wanda and Veronika Marsman. 2010. "The Association of Black Social Workers (ABSW): A model of empowerment practice." In *Structural social work in action: Examples from practice,* ed. Steven F. Hick, Heather I. Peters, Tammy Corner, and Tracy London. Toronto: Canadian Scholars' Press.

Thomas Bernard, Wanda, Lydia Lucas-White, and Dorothy Moore. 1993. "Triple jeopardy: Assessing life experiences of Black Nova Scotian women from a social work perspective." *Canadian Social Work Review,* 10(2) (Summer).

Tikkun Magazine. 2010. "Network of spiritual progressives." ⟨http://www.tikkun.org/⟩.

Todd, Sarah. 2006. "Social work and sexual and gender diversity." In *Social work in Canada: An introduction,* 2nd ed., ed. Steven F. Hick. Toronto: Thompson Educational Publishing.

Townson, Monica. 2009. "Canada's women on their own are the poorest of the poor." *CCPA Monitor,* 16(5). Ottawa: Canadian Centre for Policy Alternatives.

Trans Youth Family Allies. 2009. "TYFA resources for educators: Executive summary: Harsh realities – the experiences of transgender youth in our public schools." ⟨http://www.imatyfa.org/resources-index.html⟩.

Vaillancourt, Yves, François Aubry, Muriel Kearney, Luc Thériault, and Louise Tremblay. 2004. "The Contribution of the social economy towards healthy social policy reforms in Canada: A Quebec viewpoint," in *Social determinants of health: Canadian perspectives,* ed. Dennis Raphael. Toronto: Canadian Scholar's Press.

Vernon, Ayesha and John Swain. 2002. "Theorizing divisions and hierarchies: Towards a commonality of diversity?" *Disability studies today,* ed. Colin Barnes, Mike Oliver, and Len Barton. Cambridge: Polity Press.

Voices of Youth in Care. 2004. "Manifesto for change: A service user speaks." In *A Collection of Memoirs, documentaries and writings,* CD co-ordinated by Rachel Kronick, Montreal, CKUT, Radio McGill, 2004, CD hour 4.

Wa Cheew Wapaguunew Iskew (Peacock, Carolyn). 2009. "Practicing from the Heart." In *Walking this path together: Anti-racist and anti-oppressive child welfare practice,* ed. Susan Strega and Sohki Aski Esquao (Jeannine Carrière). Black Point, N.S.: Fernwood Publishing.

Walker, Peter. 2007. "Trust, risk and control within an indigenous non-indigenous social service partnership." *International Journal of Social Welfare*, 16.

Waterfall, Barbara. 2006. "Native peoples and child welfare practices: Implicating social work education." In *Canadian social policy: Issues and perspectives*, 4th ed., ed. Anne Westhues. Waterloo, Ont.: Wilfrid Laurier University Press.

Wehbi, Samantha, ed. 2004. *Community organizing against homophobia and heterosexism: The world through rainbow-colored glasses*. Binghamton, N.Y.: Haworth Press.

Wehbi, Samantha. 2009. "Deconstructing motivations: Challenging international placements." *International Social Work*, 52(1).

Welsh, Moira. 2004. "Nursing homes to face major changes: $191M yearly for 2,000 extra staff – new tougher laws to prevent abuse." *The Toronto Star*, May 11.

Wilson, Dan and David Macdonald. 2010. "Income gap for Aboriginal peoples stubbornly high: Report." News Release from National Office. Ottawa: Canadian Centre for Policy Alternatives. April 8 ⟨www.policyalternatives.ca/newsroom/news-releases⟩.

Wilson, Shawn. 2008. *Research is ceremony: Indigenous research methods*. Black Point, N.S.: Fernwood Publishing.

Wright, Kristie, Shahina Sayani, Andrea Zammit, and Purnima George. 2010. "Envisioning structural social work practice: The Case of the grassroots youth collaborative." In *Structural social work: Examples from practice*, ed. Steven F. Hick, Heather I. Peters, Tammy Corner, and Tracy London. Toronto: Canadian Scholars' Press.

Wright, Ronald. 2000. *Stolen continents: Conquest and resistance in the Americas*. London: Phoenix Press.

Yalnizyan, Armine. 2009. "Income inequality is not sustainable economically for any of us." *CCPA Monitor*, 16(1). Ottawa: Canadian Centre for Policy Alternatives.

Yalnizyan, Armine and Seth Klein. 2009. "Poverty reduction strategy: Alternative budget plan would narrow the income gap." *CCPA Monitor*, 15(9). Ottawa: Canadian Centre for Policy Alternatives.

Yalnizyan, Armine and Charles Pascal. 2004. "Our manufactured health-care crisis." *CCPA Monitor*, 11(5). Ottawa: Canadian Centre for Policy Alternatives.

Yee, June Ying and Gary C. Dumbrill. 2002. "Whiteout: Looking for race in Canadian social work practice." In *Multicultural social work in Canada*, ed. John Graham and Al Krenawi. Toronto: Oxford University Press.

Zijad, Delic. 2010. "Islamophobia: The disease that threatens healthy citizenship." *Friday Magazine*, 13(9), Feb. 26. Canadian Islamic Congress. ⟨www.canadianislamiccongress.com⟩.

Zinn, Howard. 1994. *You can't be neutral on a moving train*. Boston: Beacon Press.